ADVANCE PRAISE FOR
SUPERCOMMUNICATOR

"If you stopped needing to communicate in 1998, you don't need this book. The rest of us do. . . . From the brave new world of multimedia and infographics, to timeless lessons on finding a human voice and telling a compelling story, Frank Pietrucha's book is your modern primer in communication."

—Paul Smith, author, *Lead with a Story*

"*Supercommunicator* reminds us of the basics of communication: know your audience, your topic, and your message. At the same time, it emphasizes how dramatically the twenty-first century has changed the ways in which people hear and process information, and it guides us in how to adapt our communication styles for today's audiences."

—Candace Fleming, CIO and VP of Technology, Columbia University

"An era of complexity demands a fresh legion of communicators that can tame it. Frank Pietrucha calls them "supercommunicators." They are professionals who are able to organize and synthesize vast amounts of data, and then transform them into compelling written and visual stories that their audiences can understand. With its mixture of short essays, case studies, and practical advice, this book is a neat resource for those interested in communicating with simplicity, clarity, and depth."

—Alberto Cairo, University of Miami, author, *The Functional Art*

"Frank Pietrucha serves up as many facets of communications as Baskin-Robbins does flavors. Without lecturing, he illustrates how to attract and educate audiences via ever more complex communication tools. . . . Is it a bird? Is it a plane? No, but it's a book that ought to be required reading for every student or professional at any stage in his or her career."

—John J. Seng, CEO, Spectrum Science Communications and Chair, GLOBALHealthPR

SUPERCOMMUNICATOR

Explaining the Complicated So Anyone Can Understand

FRANK J. PIETRUCHA

AMACOM

American Management Association
New York • Atlanta • Brussels • Chicago • Mexico City •
San Francisco • Shanghai • Tokyo • Toronto • Washington, D.C.

This publication is designed to provide accurate and authoritative information in regard to the subject matter covered. It is sold with the understanding that the publisher is not engaged in rendering legal, accounting, or other professional service. If legal advice or other expert assistance is required, the services of a competent professional person should be sought.

LIBRARY OF CONGRESS CATALOGING-IN-PUBLICATION DATA
Pietrucha, Frank J.
  Supercommunicator : explaining the complicated so anyone can understand / Frank J. Pietrucha.
    pages cm
  Includes index.
  ISBN-13: 978-0-8144-3368-3 (pbk.)
  ISBN-10: 0-8144-3368-5 (pbk.)
  1. Communication of technical information. 2. Communication. 3. Business communication.
I. Title.
  T10.5.P54 2014
  302.2--dc23
                          2013041832

ABOUT AMA
American Management Association (www.amanet.org) is a world leader in talent development, advancing the skills of individuals to drive business success. Our mission is to support the goals of individuals and organizations through a complete range of products and services, including classroom and virtual seminars, webcasts, webinars, podcasts, conferences, corporate and government solutions, business books, and research. AMA's approach to improving performance combines experiential learning—learning through doing—with opportunities for ongoing professional growth at every step of one's career journey.

.

Printing number

10 9 8 7 6 5 4 3

Dedicated to my parents, Frank Anthony and Dorothy Bol Pietrucha...

To my dad, the artist, who encouraged me to reach for the sky,

And my mom, the banker, who taught me to keep both feet firmly planted on the ground.

Contents

Introduction: An Elephant Named Digital Communication   1

PART I
HOW DIGITAL TECHNOLOGY IS CHANGING COMMUNICATION   7

1. Deliver Meaning   11
2. The Dawn of the Multimedia Age   19
3. What Is Multimedia?   25
4. Digital Media Changes the Way We Experience Information   37
5. Finding the Right Medium to Deliver Your Content   43

PART II
KNOW THY AUDIENCE   49

6. Why Smart People Misread Their Audiences   53
7. Learning About Your Audience   57
8. Addressing Multiple Audiences   65
9. Researching Cultural Issues   71

PART III
KNOW THY SUBJECT 75

10. If You Are Not a Subject Expert … 79
11. Advice for Content Experts 83

PART IV
SIMPLICITY AND CLARITY 87

12. Simplify Your Content 91
13. But Don't Oversimplify 97
14. Focus on Clarity 101

PART V
GUIDELINES FOR EFFECTIVE COMMUNICATION 105

15. Supercommunicator Basic Guidelines 109

PART VI
HUMANIZE YOUR COMMUNICATIONS 119

16. Find Your Human Voice 121
17. Speaking Human … Without the Human 127
18. It's Story Time! 131
19. Testimonials: A Supercommunicator's Win-Win 141
20. Case Examples That Make Learning Real 145
21. What Not to Do When Speaking Human 151

PART VII
GETTING AN AUDIENCE TO CARE 155

22. The Power of Personalization 157
23. Rational Thinking Isn't Always the Rational Choice 161

PART VIII
BUILDING BLOCKS AND ANALOGIES   167

24. Building a Path to Comprehension   169
25. The Power of Comparison   177
26. Analogies in a Professional Setting   185

PART IX
VISUAL AND INTERACTIVE   191

27. More than a Garnish   195
28. Quality and Integrity in Design   201
29. Visuals for Presentations   209
30. Let Your Audience Explore   219
31. Your Role as a Supercommunicator   225

A Debt of Gratitude   233
Notes   237
Index   245
About the Author   257

SUPERCOMMUNICATOR

An Elephant Named Digital Communication

This book started out as a "how-to guide" on communicating complicated topics . . . but something happened along the way.

My plan was to share with you my experiences as a communicator specializing in helping clients explain subjects that most would consider difficult or complex. My job is to make sure my clients' concepts are articulated in a way that brings meaning to their ideas and turns the complicated into something understandable. I work with engineers, scientists, economists, and others who deal with big numbers and big concepts, and I assist them in molding their hard-to-comprehend content into something that nonspecialists, the rest of us, can readily grasp. Too often, potentially great projects are dismissed by management, investors, and regulators simply because those decision makers can't understand their value. But the communication of complicated ideas isn't just a corporate problem. Many of us shut out new

ideas in business and at home when there's even a hint that the concept at hand may be too hard to figure out. Opportunities can be
missed and bad things can happen when content originators don't
explain their subjects in easy-to-understand language.

There's more need for my services than you can probably imagine.
My career has been anything but boring: I have helped engineers at
NASA communicate the Agency's need for information technology; I
developed campaigns to help officials improve their economies on
behalf of George Washington University; and I enabled dozens of
startups to simplify their message for investors and potential clients.
It's always rewarding to help organizations with interesting but complicated ideas explain themselves to the rest of the world.

To broaden the book beyond my own experiences and advice, I
interviewed other professional communicators to see what they considered their "best practices" in communicating the complicated. I met
some fascinating people along the way, and all was going fine—but the
more interviews I conducted, and the more research I did, the more I
realized the scope of the book needed to change. There was an elephant in the room with me, staring at me all day as I worked. Despite
his mammoth size, I carried on like he wasn't using up all the oxygen
in the room. But I couldn't ignore him any longer. He got too big and
made too much noise. I knew I had to acknowledge his presence even
if that meant changing the focus of the book. That elephant is named
digital communication.

At the most basic level, new digital tools make it easier for people
to access complicated subjects. The recent rise in the use of video,
audio, graphics, and interactive features gives content producers the
ammunition to fight battles in the name of knowledge. In this book, I
will use the term *multimedia* to describe a broad range of communication tools. Multimedia means any type of presentation that uses both
words and graphics. It can be as simple as a poster board with text and
a photograph. Or it can be something more compelling—like data
visualization, which offers us new ways to turn boring data into effective content. Infographics, for example, help us see meaning in things

we couldn't otherwise comprehend. And the Internet—which has made all of these tools more accessible—has altered not only how we get information but also how we express ourselves. Digital technology is rewiring our brains and reshaping how we communicate.

What I learned from my years of explaining complicated subjects is still extremely useful. All that I do to make technical topics easier for others—from audience awareness to simplicity in writing to employing attention-grabbing techniques—is still essential to my role as a communicator. But digital technology is changing the rules about how we apply our skills in a transforming world. Most of us need to do more thinking about digital technology and how to strategically incorporate it into our communication efforts. No matter what new features come our way, we still need to be mindful of the classic techniques that have been employed by writers and orators for centuries. Winners in the transition from print thinking to digital expression will be people who can transfer classic communication styles to a uniquely modern paradigm.

Professionals "should learn to communicate with ordinary people. Then the common people wouldn't be so common."[1]
—JOHN L. BECKLEY

It's important for businesses to articulate who they are and what they do with clarity and meaning in order to survive in a society where complicated material is abundant. Our world is on the cusp of radical change as biotechnology, artificial intelligence, nanotechnology, synthetic biology, and other advancements come of age. The digital revolution breaks the centuries-old tradition of knowledge being a precious commodity held by an elite few. The democratization of information is happening. Our job as communicators is to make a larger percentage of our population aware of these game-changing advancements. The digital age is about inclusion, not exclusivity. The Internet gives us the power to unite disparate people, and communicators are needed to use the technology to bring meaning to those who seek information.

And so, this book is not just about successfully communicating the complicated, but doing so in this new and exciting digital age. It is increasingly the case that failing to investigate the options available in our new Internet-charged world and embrace them in our daily work can cripple careers. Individuals who can incorporate new features into their skill set are more likely to thrive. In that spirit, I aim to illustrate what the digital revolution means to those of us who communicate.

I came up with the term *supercommunicator* to describe forward-thinking professionals who can apply classic writing, speaking, and content development skills to a mindset befitting the quickly evolving millennium. Modeled after the Greek god Hermes, who translated and delivered messages from Mount Olympus to earthbound mortals, supercommunicators make sense of an increasingly complicated world. They turn technical *Geek-Speak* into everyday, layman's language, enabling real people to see big-picture scenarios they might otherwise miss. Their efforts make intimidating ideas less frightening in an era of overabundant input. Most importantly, they are knowledgeable about new digital tools that help make learning easier—and can effortlessly incorporate them into their work.

***

If you need to communicate as part of your professional responsibilities, I hope you will join me in adopting a supercommunicator mindset.

BIG-PICTURE IDEAS, PRACTICAL ADVICE

This is both a *how-to* book and a *big-idea* book. You can improve your ability to communicate complicated ideas as you learn from the tips and techniques explained in the following pages. Whether your professional interests have to do with targeting audiences, using new digital tools, or making changes to your writing style, I'm confident you'll find solutions you can make your own. I've also included numerous case examples and interesting stories to help you see how these techniques can be applied to real-life challenges.

If you're a business or government leader, this book is for you. Every day great ideas fall by the wayside because they weren't properly explained. To be successful in an increasingly competitive marketplace, you need to articulate a clear and easy-to-understand message to all relevant parties. Financiers, management, stockholders, board members, regulators, clients, analysts, and employees all demand clarity from you—and these days, business people don't have the interest or patience to wade through ineffective communications. Supercommunicating executives know how to touch their public with lucidity and conviction, or at least how to manage other people who can do this for them. This book aims to arm you with their tools and clue you in to their best practices.

If you're a communicator—and that's a broad area—this book is also for you. Whether you work for a public relations agency, marketing department, or news organization, or you develop content elsewhere, it's in your interest to see how the field of communications is responding to dramatic changes in technology and society. What's happening at lightning speed in the world today affects the way you will do your job, more than you may realize and very soon. This book is intended to provide you with a big-picture view and awareness of communications today, along with a bounty of useful, insightful ideas.

USE YOUR JUDGMENT

To make the best use of *Supercommunicator*, please use your judgment. This book offers advice everyone should consider, but there are also tips that may not be applicable to all situations. "Clarity," for example, is something everyone who writes or speaks in business, science, and technology should know about. However, "storytelling," another topic we'll explore, can be an excellent tool to explain complicated ideas—for the right audience. The method you use to speak to a crowd of creatives might not be suited for a rigid, button-down audience, and vice versa.

Ideally, most of my suggestions would be embraced by a world ready to communicate complicated content more effectively. But in actuality, some organizations cling to the formality and stilted ways of yesteryears. Your judgment is necessary to determine the applicability of content in this book to your situation. It may be worthwhile for you to be a maverick and forge a new communication style for your company—yet, if you go too far it could mean professional trouble. When possible, I do my best to point out what approaches to use for which audiences, but do be mindful of these matters on your own.

How Digital Technology Is Changing Communication

Words, pictures, graphics, and symbols—the very shape of content—is evolving before our eyes. The written word isn't going away, but it is being transformed. The days of straight running text on paper as our principal means of expressing ideas and delivering information are numbered as new digital tools change our communication landscape. For some, this transformation is liberating . . . for others, it's terrorizing.

For communicators—anyone with information or ideas to share—today is a period of transition. We can now *show* audiences insights that previously could only be explained with words. Tools born of the Internet allow us to manipulate data into forms that can bring us deeper understanding. The ease of multimedia grants even the technologically challenged the power to communicate with video, audio, and images to deliver a fuller communication experience. All good stuff, but these changes aren't likely to come easily after centuries of thinking print. Flipping the switch from print to digital requires effort on our part.

If you communicate, take note: Failure to understand new media forms and how they impact the way we write, speak, and think could leave you at a disadvantage. Conversely, embracing new digital tools—and the philosophy that drives them—can help you thrive in our hyperconnected world.

THE DIGITAL REVOLUTION CHANGES EVERYTHING IN COMMUNICATIONS. We can no longer think in terms of paper documents as our end product. The Internet is increasingly pushing more dynamic modes of communication—not just functioning as a mechanism to deliver pdf files. Multimedia engages users in a way print cannot—offering them greater insights.

THE DIGITAL REVOLUTION CHANGES NOTHING IN COMMUNICATIONS. Solid, time-tested communication skills are still an imperative. "Old school" ways to develop content are, and will always be, essential to information sharing.

THE DIGITAL REVOLUTION CHANGES EVERYTHING IN COMMUNICATIONS, YET NOTHING AT ALL. Communications is about delivering meaning. Multimedia can help us grab someone's attention. It can also enable us to deliver a more powerful learning experience by "showing" rather than "telling." But we can't depend on killer applications alone to express thoughts and share information. There has to be substance behind the style to breathe new life into content. Technology can enhance our understanding of content, but there must be solid ground beneath the gadgets and gizmos.

You may already know about some of the technologies described in the coming pages, but read with an open mind. The introductory chapters aren't so much about new tools as they're about developing the frame-of-mind to seamlessly incorporate new devices into your communication efforts. We've been busy adopting new communication tools, but have we taken the time to think about how they can best serve us?

1

Deliver Meaning

"We've been trying to get our arms around this whole remarkable reality of the advancements of digital communication," confesses Tom Becker, president of the Chautauqua Institution. New, powerful ways to reach more people with specific information, he admits, are now a "compelling reality" that must be addressed. But there's a lot at stake for Becker, who knows he needs to incorporate new technology into his programming but also must preserve Chautauqua's storied tradition of oratory and discussion. The institution has survived over a century by providing a platform for great thinkers to share ideas—and their classic format hasn't changed in all that time. The digital world, however, is knocking at Chautauqua's front door. It needs to make tough decisions about its role in a communications environment driven by technology.

Each summer, Chautauqua, a historic lakefront community in southwestern New York, plays host to more than 100,000 visitors who come to participate in arts and educational programs as well as attend its famous daily morning lecture series. Since it opened in 1874, prominent intellectuals, artists, scientists, politicians, and other great minds have gathered at this "oasis" to consider the issues of the best of human values and the enrichment of life. All morning lecturers, before and after the day Franklin D. Roosevelt took center stage, have been faced with the same challenge: They speak to an audience of 4,000 with limited use of multimedia for forty-five minutes, followed by a rigorous fifteen-minute question and answer period. But big changes are on the drawing board for the celebrated institution. In the not-too-distant future, speakers will be able to incorporate state-of-the-art multimedia into their lectures. Plans to rehabilitate the amphitheater with all the technological marvels of the Internet age are underway.

The proposed technological upgrades at Chautauqua are sleek, but Becker has to make sure their inclusion doesn't detract from the human experience of people coming together to discuss and think through ideas. "I think our environment is as important today as it was in 1874 when we were founded," Becker comments. "But in 1874 it had to do with what is now accomplished by the digital age . . . access to information. People needed gatherings like this as a way to acquire access to science, history, and public affairs. That's not our problem today. The gathering at a human scale in this place today is vitally important for different reasons than we first gathered."

"Our ethic here," he continues, "is to go into the quality of the argument itself. We ask our audiences to continue to develop their critical thinking about how someone presents a problem, defines it, lays out their proposed solution, and then gives the evidence as to why that would work and then evaluates the reasoning behind all of that."

Becker believes Chautauqua's model for the next century isn't about competing with technology to deliver quantities of information, but to help individuals place important issues in context and help them make better sense of the world around them. Using new technological tools to move forward is great, as long as we take the time to reflect about the message. Effective communications promote reflective reasoning by helping people open their minds to dig past the superficial and find deeper meaning.

The digital age is about information. Finding new ways to obtain, analyze, and share data is essential. Providing information to audiences clearly is the essence of what we do as communicators, but shouldn't we aim higher? Our mandate should be to strive not just to deliver information, but also to bring meaning to our audience through thoughtful explanation.

The lessons we learned in school, like how to research material, select relevant facts, then logically assemble our findings, remain essential in our information-drenched world. The ability to detect patterns and marshal disjointed bits of data is even more crucial in the digital age. Information needs to be contextualized and frameworks need to be established to bring audiences references and grounding. The abundance of data—both hurtling through cyberspace and in our everyday, pen-and-paper lives—can easily push us into *infomageddon*— a chasm where content is plentiful, but meaningless.

Too many of us forget to deliver meaning in our communication efforts. We rush to produce presentations and reports, focusing on facts and figures we believe essential to state our case, but in our haste we neglect to tell our audiences why these data are important. The old adage "He couldn't see the forest for the trees" comes to mind. We get so wrapped up in the abundance of information available that we lose sight of the simple takeaway. Only stepping back and sorting through each element will help us to regain perspective.

Specialists—people like engineers, scientists, and Ph.D. types— are often the worst offenders. Some of our smartest citizens are often at a loss for how to explain their specialized, often intricate subject matter to the rest of us. Their communication problems can be vastly improved by understanding how to spotlight the deeper meaning among all of the details.

With so many shiny new multimedia objects vying for our attention, it's easy to get caught up in the excitement of the sizzle and forget meaning. But let's remember . . . it's our message audiences need to remember, not our tactics. Use new tools to help people develop a deeper understanding that encourages them to think about your subject. Multimedia can be tremendously effective in helping you explain the complicated. But leave your audience blinded by thought-provoking ideas and dialogue, not the dazzle of your presentation.

Failure to Deliver Meaning: The Higgs Boson Case

How much do you know about the Higgs boson? The elementary particle confirmed to exist in 2013 was big news around the world. Physicists waited a half-century for this event. The media told us the breakthrough was huge. If you read about the discovery, can you tell me why it was epic?

My learning experience with the Higgs boson wasn't so much a revelation about physics, but about how many communicators fail to deliver meaning to their audiences. I read several articles and blogs that described great zeal over the discovery. Yet in some of the world's most respected media outlets, no reporter or blogger could explain why this particle was a paradigm changer in a manner I could understand.

It bothered me that I couldn't comprehend this story. I wondered . . . am I just that dense when it comes to physics? Or are these articles ineffective? So I surveyed the morning regulars at Peregrine Espresso here on Capitol Hill in Washington, DC, to see if any of them got it. A group of mostly middle-age-plus guys, and an occasional brave woman or two, meet there most mornings to discuss politics, sports, relationships, and just about anything on anyone's mind.

This collection of college professors, lawyers, international aid workers, government executives, a few random politicos, and a social worker turned handyman aren't shy about expressing their opinions. If this group of highly educated, well-informed latte drinkers didn't grasp the significance of the Higgs, I figured, most of America wouldn't, either. My suspicions were confirmed: Everyone had heard about the discovery, but no one comprehended it. Later, a physicist I interviewed for this book, who chose not to be identified, told me he estimates that probably less than a percent of Americans can speak knowledgeably about the Higgs boson or why it's important.

Frustrated, I dedicated a couple of days to doing nothing but research to discover the mystery of the famous particle. I read and re-read dozens of articles and blogs to see if I could find a glimmer of light that would lead to some low level of understanding. But in everything I read, nothing seemed to bring meaning to me. I felt either assaulted by physics jargon or underwhelmed by fluff. Nothing was helping me figure out why this was a big discovery and why I should care about it. It doesn't matter to me if physicists are excited about confirming a theory; I wanted to know what's in it for me! Why should I care about the Higgs boson?

If I had been asked to write about the Higgs boson at this point in time, my summary would look something like this:

> *Scientists are celebrating because the discovery of the Higgs boson confirms that the Standard Model of particle physics is consistent with what they hypothesized. Physicists use this theory to explain how the universe works. The confirmation of the Higgs boson's existence can help them better understand how the Big Bang occurred.*

That summary may be factually correct. But we could do much better. My readers can take away from this that the discovery is an important scientific breakthrough, but there's nothing there that is particularly meaningful to them.

After hours of research, I finally came across a video clip of Columbia University physicist and best-selling author Brian Greene

lecturing on the Higgs boson at the Aspen Ideas Festival (like a West-
ern Chautauqua). Eighteen minutes into the twenty-minute video pre-
sentation, he said something that finally resonated with me. The
clichéd light bulb went off over my head. Greene said that the Higgs
boson discovery has no practical implications of which scientists are
aware—yet. That piece of information gave me some relief. I'd been
waiting for something tangible to help me comprehend this revela-
tion . . . and it turns out there is none—just yet. We humans crave tan-
gibility.

Ironically, it was the understanding of the lack of tangibility that
finally created the spark that helped me grasp the enormity of this
discovery. Greene, apparently a supercommunicator, eloquently
explained: Sometimes we need to "wait for theoretical discoveries to
turn into practical applications."[1] He drew an analogy to the discov-
ery of quantum mechanics back in the 1920s and 1930s. Apparently,
quantum mechanics was as abstract to people back then as we find
the Higgs boson today. But Greene explained that quantum mechan-
ics helped scientists and engineers in unprecedented ways—they
understand more about molecules, atoms, and subatomic particles.
The discovery of quantum mechanics ultimately led to the invention
of things that today we couldn't imagine living without. Take, for
instance, personal computers and cell phones. Anything with a circuit
wouldn't have been possible without the discovery of quantum
mechanics.

With this example I now understood that the Higgs could soon
usher in a new era of scientific understanding that could lead to more,
greater technological breakthroughs.

Now, let me try again to rewrite the summary. This time with
meaning:

> *The discovery of the elusive Higgs boson confirms the the-*
> *ory scientists have been using to understand how the uni-*
> *verse works. Physicists are celebrating this breakthrough*
> *because it can lead to other significant findings like the dis-*

covery of quantum mechanics did almost a century ago. Quantum mechanics led to the invention of many of the twentieth century's most notable technologies . . . like cell phones, computers, and even the atomic bomb. The discovery of the Higgs boson could be equally important . . . if not more so. It can lead to innovations we can't yet imagine.

By linking the Higgs boson discovery to tangible examples that resulted from the discovery of quantum mechanics, I was finally able to grasp some of the significance of this highly hyped science story. The discovery of the Higgs boson is possibly much bigger than opening the door to new technologies, but this simple comparison helped me put the Higgs discovery into a context I could comprehend. From here I could grow to understand more about this great physics discovery. Finally, I found meaning.

2

The Dawn of the Multimedia Age

The early digital era—our very recent past—has been about transplanting offline material online. That's in the process of changing. Jeff Stanger, founder of the Center for Digital Information, says many of us use the Internet to deliver the same kind of content we've generated for generations—it just so happens that we're transmitting them electronically. We write documents, possibly add a few graphic embellishments, save them as Word, PowerPoint, or pdf files, and then post them to a website or send them through cyberspace to another destination as an email attachment. When the receiving or requesting party opens the document, that person gets a static document—like any other document produced over the past several hundred years . . . it just happened to have been sent electronically—not by mail or messenger. The Internet to date, says Stanger, has been largely used by content producers as a delivery mechanism, but "now we're at an inflection point to a native digital era."

The Internet can do so much more than just help us do research and transmit documents. There's an exciting world of opportunity for communicators to find new outlets of expression, and we've only just scratched the surface. Whether delivered on a website, through social media, or as an enhanced e-article or e-book, Internet-powered applications can help us see new details or gain a better perspective on subjects that would otherwise have remained opaque. Today's adventure into a new communication frontier starts with a fresh look at how we view content development. Most of us automatically think "document" when tasked with originating content. New tools and techniques, along with new attitudes, are changing all that. "Digital natives," those individuals that thought leader Marc Prensky describes as "native speakers of the digital language,"[2] are starting to express ideas and explain complicated subjects to others through more dynamic means. Digital natives are also called "Millennials," the generation making its passage into adulthood at the start of the new millennium. Confident, expressive, and open to change, these fluent speakers of the digital language take to multimedia with great ease.[3] They grew up with computers. Many of the changes underway are being driven by this demographic group. But digital native or not, it's time for you to explore multimedia's benefits if you haven't already started.

THE INTERNET IS REWIRING OUR BRAINS

Quantitatively speaking, we are the most informed generation in history. As trillions of bytes of information in cyberspace wait for us, ready to pulse through our fingertips at the command of a click, we are actively rewiring our brains. Stimulation, the kind we're getting from our daily data feasts, is changing our brain structure through neuroplasticity. The Internet is, in fact, changing our brains; this isn't an urban myth, but scientific reality.

There's no need to worry about changes to our brain from a physiological standpoint, but understanding its evolution is essential to anyone who communicates. As writer Nicholas Carr points out, our "calm, focused, undistracted linear mind is being pushed aside by a new kind of mind that wants and needs to take in information in short, disjointed, often overlapping bursts . . ."[4] In a short span of only a couple of decades, the Internet has turned careful, deliberate readers into information hunters. Like hungry predators, we charge forward into our devices demanding an instantaneous fix only to lurch away moments later searching for more prey. This is very different from a generation ago, when people sat passively in libraries carefully reading books uninterrupted from start to finish.

Words printed on paper have always facilitated concentrated and sustained attention and thought. We were like content sponges soaking up knowledge like a puddle on the floor. We read in a linear manner, from left to right, and reflected on the content. Our role was passive; we sat, read, and pondered. We discussed content with classmates or colleagues, but would rarely interact with the author him or herself. Our brains got very comfortable over a half millennium or so with this static means of acquiring and sharing information.

The story of the singularly focused scholar, however, is quickly, and, most suddenly, becoming ancient history. The Internet encourages "a more distributed and plastic form of thinking,"[5] leaving us new ways to experience information. Power scanning, instead of deep reading, is something we all do. Even academics confess to engaging in selective reading. *Networked journal articles*, rich interactive representations of current scientific knowledge, for example, enable academics to pursue "rapid and high-volume strategic reading."[6] This would have been unthinkable a generation ago among the academic elite. But with so much content readily available online, who has time to read through everything thoroughly? We've taught ourselves how to search and edit information at a glance with amazing efficiency. We go online, get what we want . . . and we get out.

While the rewiring of our brains is already having an impact on today's researchers, the greatest changes are occurring among the people who will be presiding over our burgeoning digital kingdom in the near future. Hyperconnected digital natives will reap the rewards of the Internet's bounty as they hopscotch from one idea to the next, fueling their creative pursuits. As they come to regard the Internet as their external brain, experts tell us, today's youth will not only be more expressive but will also be "nimble analysts" and effective "decision makers."[7] But all is not perfect in our digital future; there are downsides to an Internet-powered brain. These same experts warn us that our constantly connected youth will more likely jump to make quick, shallow choices in their constant quest for instant gratification.

Digital Native or Not— Jump on the Bandwagon

Carole Al-Kahouaji is a curriculum development pro and a grandmother. She knows that you need to embrace new digital means of expression to remain relevant, regardless of your age. As head of school at Rock Creek International School in Washington, DC, she pioneered programs to engage students in multimedia at a tender young age. Grammar school students built websites and developed digitally driven presentations—often in two languages—as homework assignments. The young people, she notes, take naturally to the new digital tools, but that doesn't mean the rest of us should become digital slackers. "It may not be as intuitive to older people, but it's still necessary," she says. "Keeping an open mind and keeping up with what's out there is essential," if you want to communicate effectively in the twenty-first century.

Al-Kahouaji is not alone in her observation. Communicators need to comprehend and apply new tools and styles to remain current. "Having a quick, snappy, powerful way to convey information is an imperative these days," says Lee Rainie, who studies the habits of

Millennials and other digital age citizens at the Pew Research Center's Internet & American Life Project. "Lots of professional organizations are moving toward short crisp videos . . . two or three minutes with a human face and some simple infographics . . . It's another way for knowledge-based businesses to disseminate complicated information."

For more information on Pew's Internet & American Life Project please visit: http://www.pewinternet.org/Topics/Demographics/Digital-Divide.aspx?typeFilter=5.

CHAPTER

3

What Is Multimedia?

Journalists have been dabbling with multimedia for years. Steps ahead of the book business in embracing new digital forms, news organizations see multimedia's potential to tell stories with greater zip while enhancing the quality of their reporting. After years of experimentation, they've figured out how digital applications can add value to a reader's experience. This is evidenced by a December 2012 feature in *The New York Times*—one that critics regard as a turning point in digital age storytelling.

"Snow Fall: The Avalanche at Tunnel Creek" won the 2012 Pulitzer Prize for Feature Writing, thanks to its "evocative narrative," which was "enhanced by its deft integration of multimedia elements."[8] Many agree "Snow Fall" was a good story on its own merit, but the way it was told was revolutionary. A week after it was released on the

Times site, over 2.9 million visitors—many of them new to the venerable news organization—had tuned to a compelling story that exemplifies what digital-age communication should look like.

The story focuses on sixteen highly experienced skiers and snowboarders who gathered at the summit of Cowboy Mountain in Washington State for an outdoor experience none of them would forget—and three of them would not survive. An abundance of fresh snow—the arrival of which they all cheered earlier in the day—turned deadly as a chunk 200 feet across, 3 feet deep, and weighing millions of pounds broke free from the mountaintop. The snow cascaded down Tunnel Creek, an unpatrolled "powder stash," at over 70 miles per hour, steamrolling everything in its way for 2,650 feet. The avalanche snapped sturdy trees like flimsy toothpicks and picked up five skiers in its path. Only two survived.

Well written and engaging, the series captured the attention of its readers and effectively described the awesome strength of avalanches and the perils of going *off piste*. But the *Times* feature did more: It awakened millions to a new force that had nothing to do with Mother Nature's fury. "Snow Fall" opened readers' eyes to the brilliant possibilities of multimedia as a turbo-charged communication vehicle.

More than a dozen people were enlisted to create the fifty multimedia elements used to tell this 16,000-word story, which was neither easy nor cheap to produce.[9] Arguably no other news organization had produced such an extensive multimedia experience prior to this series. Consider a sampling of the multimedia features used to tell this story:

▷ An animated visualization reveals the avalanche's path in real-time. You can see the lines skiers and boarders took down the mountain as they relate to the avalanche's deadly path.

▷ A minute-and-a-half video clip shot from skier Ron Pankey's helmet cam shows his discovery of the debris field and buried skiers at the bottom of Tunnel Creek with boarder Tim Carlson. A voice-over of an emotional Carlson is added to the video as he relives the incident.

▷ The use of various technical and design components like scrolling mechanisms, curtain effect features, and cinemagraphs provides unique graphical backdrops.[10]

▷ An animated infographic explains how two weeks of snow and hoar frost set the stage for a "perfect storm" avalanche.

▷ Professional skier Elyse Saugstad, in a videotaped recollection, tells how she survived Tunnel Creek thanks to an air bag she had stored in her backpack. She describes vividly how she was "being tossed over and over and over," equating her experience to being in a washing machine.

▷ An animation demonstrates how Saugstad's life-saving air bag worked.

▷ A recording of an actual 911 call offers real-time emotion from survivors.

The abundance of multimedia tools provided readers with a deeper appreciation of the tragedy and better educated them about the power of avalanches—much better than a mere print piece could ever do. Photography and animation of the mountain helped readers visualize the event geographically. The post-event interviews added credibility to the piece—making it feel more real. The weather-related infographic promoted a better understanding of how avalanches occur.

VIDEO AND AUDIO

Video and audio clips are powerful multimedia tools—and probably among the easiest for novices to incorporate into their communication efforts. Video and audio can be shot on a mobile phone, edited on site, and posted in a matter of minutes—all by an eight-year-old. These vehicles can enliven otherwise staid pieces—offering readers welcome relief from tedium—but they also provide us with a dynamic means to *show* rather than *explain* complicated topics.

Video's growth is explosive—just look at the success of video sharing website YouTube. Billions log on daily in fifty-four different languages for entertainment, information, and instruction. YouTube, like all video, is a force not a fad, but despite its widespread online presence, the use of clips is still in its infancy when it comes to business communication. You don't often find a video clip in a company's strategic plan, for example. We've been increasingly using these tools to communicate in popular culture, but we're really just scratching the surface of what can be done with audio and video when it comes to the kind of communication most of us do on a regular basis.

STILL IMAGES AND GRAPHICS

The term *still images* refers to just about anything visual that is not animated, interactive, or videotaped. This can include photography, illustrations, charts, graphs—just as long as they aren't moving or in some way interacting with the reader.

Still images and graphics have been in existence for as long as we can remember: think cave drawings. You probably already use some kind of graphics in your daily work, such as charts and graphs or maybe clip art or photography, to communicate your messages. Today's communicators need to know how to use them more effectively in our reshaped digital world. Graphic communication is a booming field. Much of what was written in the past is now being presented visually.

ANIMATION

The illusion of movement is an effective way to capture an audience's attention. Communicators use animation to tell stories or inform their audiences in a way video, audio, still images, and text cannot. Animation, like video, can be especially helpful when explaining a process or when elaborating on a topic that needs to be shown or demonstrated. Animation can be pricey, making it a reach for some communicators. But new technology is putting animation tools into the hands of regular folks. You no longer need to work for Pixar to generate a reasonable product.

Examples of successful animations are easy to find on YouTube. Seattle-based Common Craft has earned worldwide recognition thanks to its production of stop-action animation videos, which use white boards and paper cutouts to explain a variety of topics that non-specialists may find difficult to comprehend. Learn about cloud computing, how to borrow money, or how to prepare an emergency plan. Members can access their library of ready-made videos designed to introduce complex subjects in about three minutes.

The Royal Society for the Encouragement of Arts, Manufactures and Commerce, or RSA, which calls itself an "enlightenment organization," frequently shares ideas from its events as animation clips in an effort to "revolutionize the world of knowledge visualization."[11] You've probably seen its animations. They always include a hand holding a magic marker drawing visuals "in real time" onto a white board highlighting remarks given by thought leaders such as writer Dan Pink or education guru Sir Ken Robinson.

DATA VISUALIZATION

An explosion of evocative new media is quickly coming of age in the new millennium. *Visualization* is the buzzword for anything that helps us *see* data, information, or knowledge in a new light. Visualization builds on classic multimedia, but imagination, an abundant supply of data, and computer power have given birth to exciting new forms. All visualizations—whether they are static, animated, or interactive—seek to marry aesthetic form with functionality to yield insights that take us beyond basic comprehension. Vivid colors and eye-catching images are usually part of the data visualization experience.

Visualizations come in many forms—they could be static infographics that provide a snapshot of information you might find in a newspaper or a jaw-dropping animated display of scientific data projected onto a hyper-wall. There are many flavors of visualizations—and many of them overlap, making them difficult to distinguish or classify. What's important is awareness of the variety of different tools for communicators to use to explain complicated content.

Leading research institutions, corporations, and news media organizations have been the front-runners in this exciting field. In many cases, visualizations are produced to help analysts see their data from a different perspective. It just so happens that what helps the analysts see more clearly can also help other audiences experience a subject more fully. Much of the data visualization being done today is conducted to advance scientific research (like NASA), fight crime (like the FBI), and monitor credit card usage trends (like Visa), but that's just the start. Data visualization enables all of these groups to dig deep and pull out insights that help them see meaning.

INFOGRAPHICS

Presenting complex information quickly and clearly is the goal of information graphics, or infographics. Take your information, your data, or whatever knowledge you want to communicate, and package it in an appealing visual that concisely gets your point across.

Infographics have been around for centuries but have found greater popularity since they've been retooled, reshaped, and repurposed in the last couple of decades. Infographics gained popularity in the 1980s with the launch of *USA Today*, a North American daily priding itself on making news stories easy to digest. Readers found their "snapshots" of bite-size chunks of information engaging . . . and *USA Today* owner Gannett discovered they helped sell newspapers. Journalists continue to use these insightful text-, image-, and graphic-filled boxes to inform readers visually—hence cutting down on excessive straight running text. Infographics can be used to complement a story or can stand alone as their own feature. Businesses have more recently incorporated them into their communication mix as a way to impart information about their organization, services, or issues more quickly.

The visual nature of infographics makes them ideal for today's computer-based communication environment. The darling of website designers, infographics help capture surfing eyes by creating a focal point in what could otherwise be a sea of lackluster text. Browsers are intrinsically drawn into the graphic and hopefully become sufficiently engaged in its content, creating a level of *stickiness*—encouraging surfers to stay on the site. Additionally, infographics are highly transportable via social media, making them easy to share.

Form Follows Function

Infographics aren't intended to be great works of art. "Most editors aren't looking for eye candy, they're looking for something that catches the attention of their audience and makes them want to pay attention," says Amy Balliett. Her Seattle-based firm, Killer Infographics, produces up to 150 infographics a month—none of which, she will proudly tell you, are museum worthy. First and foremost, infographics must bring clarity.

Many of us grew up thinking of simple graphs and charts—like bars and pies—as a great way to explain data visually. And they still are effective tools in many cases. "Graphics can and should be beauti-

ful, fun, and engaging, but not at the cost of being harder to read or decode," says University of Miami professor Alberto Cairo. "If a bar graph allows accurate comparisons, it is the right choice."

Publishing an Excel bar graph with no visual embellishments may be too draconian if it's dull and doesn't engage your audience. Spend time making your graphics more visually appealing . . . but don't overdecorate. Always preserve functionality.

Cairo offers a completely made up example to drive this point. Using fake data, he shows the difference between a graphic that is easy to read and one that is difficult to comprehend. Figure 3.1 is what he calls "the Excel awful graph" which is "ugly, boring, badly

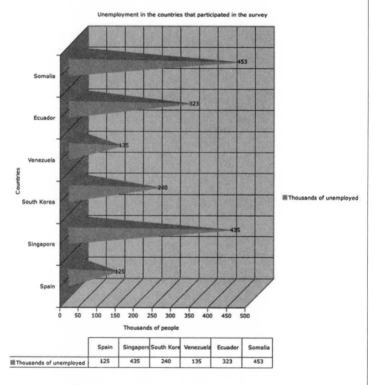

Credit: Alberto Cairo

Figure 3.1. *This example demonstrates what not to do when creating infographics. The visual enhancements, like the 3D effect, are a distraction.*

organized, and with useless 3D effect." Figure 3.2 is his makeover. See how he increased the visual appeal of the graphic without hurting the functionality. The second graphic highlights important data points and is easy on the eyes.

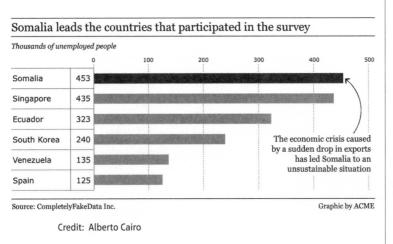

Figure 3.2. *This improved graphic is clean and functional. Create visuals that help the audience grasp your point with minimal effort.*

DATA VISUALIZATION—BIG DATA

Infographics only scratch the surface of the data visualization boom that's underway. To better understand *big data,* data sets so large and complex that you can't process or manipulate them with conventional database tools or applications, organizations are using new software to help them *visualize* the complex.[12] They take unthinkably large chunks of data and fashion them into a form that humans can comprehend. Data visualizers marry science with design to produce graphics, static and interactive, that often transcend explanation to deliver deeper meaning of complicated topics.

"Visualization is a really effective method of getting into the data and getting not just information, but getting knowledge out the other side," says visualization expert Noah Iliinsky of IBM. It's about "getting something to satisfy your own goals. You can enable a decision; you can enable an action . . . rather than just getting another number."

NASA Makes Data Come to Life

Big data means big visualizations at NASA's Goddard Space Flight Center, where the Global Modeling and Assimilation Office uses a NASA Center for Climate Simulation (NCCS) supercomputer to process over 10 million satellite observations of the atmosphere a day to predict weather conditions and study global climate. Scientists see data come to life inside the NCCS's Data Exploration Theater, where simulations are projected in high-definition on a 17- by 6-foot hyperwall composed of fifteen monitors.

Tiny bits of information on rates of precipitation, wind, humidity, ice, and other environmental conditions are transformed into simulations that bring to life images more comprehensible to the human mind than raw data. Scientists can study epic storms of the past like Hurricane Sandy and the East Coast blizzards of 2010 to observe patterns that help them improve future weather and climate forecasts.

My NASA communication colleague Jarrett Cohen gave me the full NCCS Data Exploration Theater experience on a visit to Goddard (see Figure 3.3). One of the simulations he shared was visualizations of a 220-year record of climactic activity on Planet Earth, reaching back to 1880 and forward to 2100. At Cohen's command, larger-than-life maps of the world lit up and were instantaneously populated by millions of pieces of data. Like a weatherman's display on steroids, an enormous wall showed changing sea levels, precipitation amounts, temperature variations, and even aerosol levels. The 17- by 6-foot collage of the world alone would have been worth the price of admission just because of its sheer beauty, but as 220 years of data went to work, the constantly changing map told me a compelling story of the recent history of the Earth's climate. You can read about the climate in books, in newspapers, or online, but nothing strikes an emotional chord like experiencing the data flash before you on such a grand scale and in such vivid colors.

Source: NASA

Figure 3.3 *The Data Exploration Theater at NASA's Goddard Space Flight Center in Maryland turns scientific data into works of art.*

The NCCS Data Exploration Theater delights schoolchildren and helps inform politicians—some of whom make laws that impact the environment. This visualization program does what communicators need it to do—it enables individuals to see data in a way that is meaningful to them. In this case, data visualization supplements knowledge people may already have about climate, raising their understanding of the subject to a deeper and more emotionally charged level.

But Does It Work?

"No one has done research about what sticks," Lee Rainie, director of the Pew Research Center's Internet & American Life Project, tells me. "Is an infographic better than a headline?" he asks. Then he rhetorically responds, "No one knows." This isn't exactly comforting news to those who are trying to get their arms around how to use digital media effectively. Methodologically, he tells me, surveys and interviews don't work in trying to figure out what resonates with either executives or the general population. Statistically, it's just too hard to figure out what to do to make people respond and sort out all their varied information inputs.

Supercommunicators may need to act on instinct and good judgment until researchers can figure out for us what new digital tools do to boost our ability to explain the complicated. But if you're always thinking about the importance of delivering meaning to your audience, chances are you will be far more effective in embracing multimedia. Multimedia shows lots of promise as a means to educate and inform, but users need to be thoughtful in the way they incorporate it into their communication mix.

4

Digital Media Changes the Way We Experience Information

Think about how much information can be crammed into a single web page. Perusing blocks of descriptive text, blogs, video features, interactive tools, advertisements, and response mechanisms on a single screen offers us a different experience with information than reading a page of text in a book. With so many distractions it's easy to see why our brains are rewiring. The way we consume information is changing largely because of the Internet—and that's leading to changes in other areas of our behavior.

The table on the next page presents—in a digital native–friendly manner—a view of how the Internet is changing our communications styles . . . and quite possibly our broader outlook on twenty-first-century life. The left column shows where we've come from. The classic printed book, with roots back to the Renaissance, has played a critical role in shaping our minds in the process of acquiring and exchanging information. A centuries-long tradition of static, text-heavy documents that progressed in a linear fashion grew out of the physical reality of what came off the printing press. The nature of the printed word influenced our minds to take on its characteristics. On the other side, the right column reveals descriptions of where we're heading. The digital medium gives content developers more flexibility to explain and express ideas. Multimedia opens the doors to an increasingly engaging environment stressing visual appeal, openness, as well as immediacy.

PRINT-BASED MEDIA CHARACTERISTICS	DIGITAL MEDIA CHARACTERISTICS
Static	Interactive/Dynamic
Text-heavy	Visual
Linear	Nonlinear
Defined entry point	Multiple entry points
Dense	Digestible
Broadcast	Dialogue
Opaque	Transparent

STATIC VS. INTERACTIVE/DYNAMIC

We're no longer content with words sitting on a page. Digital natives don't want to merely read about something, they want to experience it. New multimedia tools facilitate a bidirectional dialogue that engages as they inform. Users—not just readers anymore—are taking advantage of an assortment of new applications that personalize information. Interactive maps and tools that calculate numbers specific to the user's needs are just a sampling of hands-on applications that make information gathering a more dynamic experience.

TEXT-HEAVY VS. VISUAL

No one wants to read too much text. Dense paragraphs are like death sentences in the digital world, where information is increasingly communicated through visual means. Readers are naturally drawn to pictures and symbols. A smart infographic can often tell a story more efficiently than a 1,200-word article.

LINEAR VS. NONLINEAR

Digital natives want to choose how to experience content on their own—and it's usually not in a straight line. Users create their own paths to the information they want most—not depending on an author to direct them. Websites help facilitate this desire. Click on the information you want when you want it.

DEFINED ENTRY POINT VS. MULTIPLE ENTRY POINTS

The users enter into an interface at a point of their choosing. We no longer have to start with the introduction and muddle through an obligatory "up-front" discussion before getting to the meat. This feature is especially important in this era of social sharing of direct links and search as a starting point.

DENSE VS. DIGESTIBLE

Forget your 700-page tome; no one's going to read it. Short, crisp, and to the point is how digital natives like it. Boston Consulting Group's Global Marketing Director Massimo Portincaso told me they no longer expect clients or prospects to consume 10,000 to 15,000 words in one sitting. Portincaso says they have to "pre-digest" some content to reduce intellectual capital to its key points. People prefer to read no more than 1,000 words at a time.

BROADCAST VS. DIALOGUE

Social media enables digital natives to engage in conversation if not debate. This is much more appealing than reading an edict written in stone. Interactive applications, too, engage the reader in a way that feels more customized. Craft communications that speak directly to individuals, not anonymous groups of people.

OPAQUE VS. TRANSPARENT

Digital natives are big believers in transparency and, unfortunately for criminals and crooks, the Internet makes the world a more difficult place to hide. Be truthful and forthcoming. Don't present yourself as something you are not. In the words of former White House Chief Technology Officer Vivek Kundra: "A culture of closed, opaque, and secretive governance leads to corruption and ultimately to a government that doesn't work. Making data open to all, a democratizing data, empowers citizens to fight corruption."[13]

Coming Soon . . . Hopefully: Enhanced e-Books

Amazon pushed the book business into the digital era with the intro-duction of Kindle in 2007. As of 2012, over 25 percent of Americans own e-book reading devices or tablet computers—and the number is rising.[14] The next phase of this technology is enhanced e-books—dig-ital books that incorporate multimedia. They deliver a more dynamic experience for readers than conventional e-books that are essentially print books delivered over an electronic device.

Sourcebooks' Shakesperience series is a strong example of what could be—an e-book that makes the Bard's imposing works more accessible for students through a variety of multimedia features like video clips of performance scenes, an imbedded glossary of terms, and pop-up definitions.

The prospect of enhanced e-books excites digital publishers (but frightens some traditional book publishers). A number of obstacles are keeping the next generation of e-books grounded. Todd Stocke of Sourcebooks tells me readers find it difficult to navigate nonlinear books. The industry is trying to figure out how to help them "jump around" content to get to the section they want instead of progress-ing in a straightforward manner. If you are reading a guide book on Italy and want to research restaurants on the Amalfi Coast, for exam-ple, you might find it hard to get to the section you want in an e-book. If you were perusing a paperback you could easily thumb through to find out where to go for calamari in Sorrento or Positano. At this point, e-books are better suited for novels.

Money, as always, is another major factor in the accessibility of this technology. Jeremy Greenfield, editor of Digital Book World, *offers that producing enhanced e-books is an expensive undertaking with a difficult business case. "If you're a publisher . . . enhanced e-books change your entire mindset. You have a whole new distribu-tion channel and a whole new kind of business to think about." Questions publishers need to ask themselves include: What kind of content should we feature? How will we produce this? How will we move these products?*

When can we expect enhanced e-books to take off? Greenfield says children's books are already doing well. But as far as adult books go, he says industry analysts usually say "next year."

5

Finding the Right Medium to Deliver Your Content

Analytical design guru and author Edward Tufte hates Power-Point. I mean he *really* hates PowerPoint. In his 30-page essay "The Cognitive Style of PowerPoint: Pitching Out Corrupts Within,"[15] he blasts the Microsoft presentation tool in a tone that makes it sound like an evil force sent by demons to derail all communication efforts on Earth. "PowerPoint creates a cognitive style that disrupts and trivializes evidence,"[16] he writes, and that's just for starters. He goes on to trash its "obnoxious transitions and partitions,"[17] the way its slide format is sequential, and the bullet-point culture it creates. PowerPoint, he warns, provides "a smirky commercialism that turns information into a sales pitch and presenters into marketers." He even likens the presentation tool to a school play: "very loud, very slow, and very simple."[18]

I'm not ready to delete PowerPoint from my personal computer just yet, but Tufte raises some valid points about the nature of this software. He points to reports generated by NASA following the 2003 tragedy involving the space shuttle *Columbia* as his proof. *Columbia* burned up on reentry into the Earth's atmosphere following a mission. The space agency launched a thorough investigation and discovered that the accident was caused by damage to the wing's thermal protection. A series of reports were generated by NASA to explain the problem and were ultimately presented to the *Columbia* Accident Investigation Board in the form of PowerPoint slides.

The board wasn't pleased with NASA's format choice for a report of such significance. Because of the program's inherently disjointed, bullet-point style, key information was left out. Consequently, senior managers weren't able to fully comprehend the magnitude of the shuttle's problems. Tufte notes that formal engineering documents, like reports and white papers, would have been wiser, more effective formats to communicate NASA's findings.

PowerPoint has been in existence since 1990—in just over twenty years it's had a tremendous impact on the way we communicate. We've disrupted the tradition of narrative and replaced it with awkward bullet points that offer our audiences fragmented ideas. But it's popular. PowerPoint is the default presentation format for most companies. On any given day, one report discovered, there are 30 million PowerPoint presentations taking place around the world.[19] We'll examine visuals for presentations later in the book, but let's note that most people who use this software are not using it wisely. There may be a role for PowerPoint, but clearly it was the wrong choice to communicate a complicated subject like the investigation of an exploding spacecraft.

A quarter-century after its introduction, PowerPoint is by no means a cutting-edge program. But this example shows how easy it is to flock to a new format even if it's not the best solution. There are many new tools available on the market, with more coming, that promise to help us communicate more effectively. Some of them will enable us to bring greater clarity and meaning to our audiences, but that doesn't mean we should abandon what's worked for us in the past and jump to new solutions without consideration.

"Narratives" Instead of PowerPoint If You Work at Amazon

If you work for e-tail giant Amazon, don't even think about using PowerPoint. Chief executive officer Jeff Bezos believes it encourages lazy thinking and has banned the popular software program. After reading Tufte's report he allegedly insisted that Amazon employees write "narratives" instead of creating PowerPoint presentations. Amazon narratives are papers that cannot exceed six pages in length.[20]

THE BEST FIT FOR YOUR AUDIENCE

Don't be lured by the bright lights of multimedia just because they're eye-popping. Evaluate the options at hand, and only choose multimedia options if they serve your needs. Select the format that best fits your content and will resonate with your audience. Finding the right medium to deliver content is important, and with more options now available it is becoming increasingly more challenging.

But remaining stagnant and sticking with old-school communication techniques can be just as dangerous, if not more so. As Peter Reid, the vice president for strategic communications at the Woodrow Wilson International Center for Scholars, told me rather candidly: "You're simply not going to be able to survive meaningfully in this communications era if you don't learn how to get it [content] into a format that they [your audience] want it in."

The digital revolution is creating finicky information consumers. If your intended audience is somehow put off by the look or feel of your communications effort, chances are they'll move onto something else. With so much plentiful content available today, people decide very quickly where to spend their precious time. If it looks dense, boring, and offers no immediate benefit, your readers are likely to skip over it. Deciding what format to use depends on whom you're trying to reach. Conducting audience awareness, the next part of this book, is crucial as you consider your options.

Effective communicators need to understand the transformation that's underway in order to remain effective communicators. Information is being repackaged into new forms the data-weary find easier to consume. You're probably already responding to the digital revolution and are in small ways adapting your own communication style to match new trends. Maybe you're writing shorter, more active sentences or learning how to embed video onto your website. Little by little, you're probably picking up on clues from bosses, clients, or colleagues on how to make your content more appealing to twenty-first-century ears and eyes.

The move from the print mindset to the digital outlook is not one that will take place overnight. The transformation has been in the works for years and will continue to evolve over time. Smart communicators, including those of us too old to be digital natives, must pay attention to the changes occurring around us. We may not choose to learn how to employ all the new technologies or we may opt to keep a certain amount of "old school" style in some of our writings, but regardless, we must stay aware of what's happening in our new environment.

No one expects you to learn how to do it all. Communication today requires more skills than any one person can master. For big projects you'll need to work with teams of people who specialize in writing, graphic design, coding, film production, and so on. If you are leading the charge on a communications effort, however, it is your job to understand what tools are available to you so you can direct others to implement them. Additionally, as communicator, it's up to you to architect the vision for what your final product should look and feel like.

PART

II

Know Thy Audience

Different audiences need different information. I was working in Chile in the early 1990s when I first comprehended how true this is. My first assignment—just a day after arriving in Santiago—was to interview the chief technology officer of a leading telecommunications company for conference topic ideas. By phone before our meeting, I explained to him that I didn't have a background in technology but hoped to find out what "hot" telecommunications topics to include in my program.

The interview was painful. The CTO launched immediately into a detailed discussion of telecommunications technology that I could not comprehend. He attempted to explain to me, in Spanish, not my first language, how ATM works. I heard him utter *"Ahhh te eme"* and thought ATM . . . ah, like Automated Teller Machine! Why is this guy talking about cash machines as the next great thing? The Citibank around the corner already has an ATM. Only he wasn't talking banking convenience. He was attempting to explain *Asynchronous Transfer*

Mode. ATM is a network standard used by some Internet service providers (ISPs) on private, long-distance networks.[1]

I couldn't comprehend how ATM worked primarily because I didn't understand what it was needed for. After pressing him, I learned that ATM was helping in the development of what he finally called "*la supercarratera de informacíon.*" Ah, Information Superhighway. . . .[2] I had read something about that, but this was the early 1990s and we nontechnologists didn't comprehend the big forthcoming changes. Who was I to know that the CTO was attempting to explain to me how the Internet worked? Shouldn't I know what the Internet was supposed to do first before learning about how it works?

The time I spent visiting with the CTO was frustrating. He launched into a technical discussion without explaining to me the big picture of the Internet's potential. He didn't read the expressions on my face that the conversation was over my head, choosing instead to continue explaining minutiae until it became unbearable. The Chilean telecommunications conference was my first professional venture into technology, but this wouldn't be the last time an engineer would jump into details without explaining the big picture to me.

The more information you have about your audience, the greater your chances are for successfully reaching them with a meaningful message. Reading your audience is essential if you want to impart useful information to them. I don't know why the CTO couldn't make his remarks more pertinent to my needs, but I believe even the most technically savvy individuals can better explain complicated subjects to nonspecialists with a bit more awareness and effort.

Many of the communicators I interviewed for this book identified audience awareness as one of the biggest issues they believe prevents their peers from effectively sharing information. It sounds so simple—most people think they know their audiences—but most of us have sat through enough misguided presentations to know that they often don't. Investing the time to carefully consider the needs of the targeted recipients of your PowerPoint, paper, or website is essential for your communication effort to be successful.

I borrowed the title of this section from a quote I got from Dr. Anthony S. Fauci, one of the most quoted scientists in the world, who knows the importance of audience awareness. He articulated his views candidly about this issue during my interview with him. His top recommendation to communicate more effectively is to "know thy audience"; he said it like it's one of the Ten Commandments. The go-to guy for just about every medical malady and contagion known to man says this is the single most important factor when communicating complicated material. He's right—"know thy audience"—if there were a cardinal rule of communication, this would probably be it.

The director of the National Institute of Allergy and Infectious Diseases (NIAID) won't accept a speaking engagement unless he is confident he has enough information on the audience. Fauci, who's advised five different U.S. presidents on emerging health threats as well as their potential danger to entire populations, asks questions about the audience's scientific/medical background, professional responsibilities, personal experience with issues, education level, and other factors—before he starts to prepare his remarks. Finding out about your audience—and developing a clear idea about who they are and what they need—can make a crucial difference in your outreach effort.

6

Why Smart People Misread Their Audiences

Veteran astronaut Joseph P. Allen told me a NASA legend that could have easily been a deleted scene from Ron Howard's 1995 film *Apollo 13*. In this altered version of the movie, the focus isn't on astronauts Jim Lovell, Jack Swigert, and Fred Haise as they fight for their lives after an explosion cripples their spacecraft en route to the moon, but what Mission Control's Flight Director Gene Krantz, portrayed by actor Ed Harris in the film, is doing back in Houston. Described to me as "an engineer's engineer" by Allen, Krantz wasn't what you'd call media astute. A highly capable engineer, he lacked the ability to discuss his work in a manner anyone but an experienced technician could understand.

As the crisis escalated aboard *Apollo 13*, the news media demanded information from Krantz about NASA's plan to bring the astronauts home. But there was a problem: Krantz hated giving interviews. In an act of compromise he begrudgingly agreed to a one-on-one interview with a single reporter. The press corps selected a young but promising journalist who was considered knowledgeable about the *Apollo 13* mission. That reporter would serve as the media's ambassador and get from Krantz what they collectively wanted: a good story about the crisis that had captivated the nation.

The interview, however, didn't pan out as well as the media had hoped. The highly sought meeting began with Krantz pulling out two massive system diagram manuals. He opened the first tome—several inches thick—and lectured the lone reporter on the technical specifications of the modules. He described the mechanics of the operation in great detail, using jargon only an aeronautical engineer could comprehend. Using detail after detail, Krantz elaborated on the inner workings of the countless bits and pieces that powered the *Apollo* mission. He finished the first book and proceeded onto the second, equally intimidating. Krantz got further into the weeds, elaborating on facts only relevant to a specialist. The engineer didn't make eye contact once during the interview, nor did he let up for a second to allow the journalist to ask a question or say, "Slow down."

After exactly one hour the journalist raced out of the interview room and passed his colleagues as he gunned toward the exit. The other reporters stopped him and demanded to know what Krantz said in the interview. All the journalist could muster was: "They're gonna get 'em back safely."

The reporters that day learned nothing new from Krantz that was helpful in explaining plans to save the doomed astronauts. Krantz had so much information he wanted to share, but by giving the journalist so much, none of it made sense. Knowing thy audience is crucial. Understanding the audience's educational background, technological experience, and need for the information is a top priority to avoid issues like this from derailing your communication efforts.

Some smart people excel at explaining complicated content to nonspecialists, while others bomb. There are several reasons many of them find it so difficult to communicate in layman's terms:

▷ **THEY WERE TAUGHT HOW TO COMMUNICATE TO PEERS, NOT TO BROADER AUDIENCES.** Most educational systems teach specialists to communicate to like-minded people using specialized language. This might be efficient for peer-to-peer communication, but it's a hindrance when these same individuals need to communicate outside their immediate professional circle.

▷ **THEY LIVE IN A BUBBLE.** Many professionals live and breathe their science or technology. They work long hours together, socialize together, and sometimes live together. They find it hard to comprehend that others outside their world don't share their excitement for the latest gadgets or small discovery. The more engrossed they get in their profession, the more difficult it is for them to relate to folks not in their field.

▷ **THEY'RE TOO BUSY.** Professionals stretched to their limits often don't have time to customize their communications for specific audiences. Consequently, a one-size-fits-all approach is created out of necessity.   Customizing papers, web content, and presentations to select audiences is time consuming—but failure to do so can lead to a communication meltdown.

▷ **THEY'RE DRIVEN BY EGO.** We humans can't help ourselves. We want to impress our audiences with our intelligence—it's in our DNA. Many specialists often, consciously or subconsciously, use their platforms to make themselves look smart. Unfortunately, speaking or writing to impress often comes at the cost of failing to reach your audience with meaning.

If you're a technically minded individual—do any of the above points describe you? Sometimes appreciation of your issue with audience awareness can be the key that unlocks your potential as a better communicator. You can work on ways to find commonalities with your audience and develop empathy with them. You can expose yourself to people outside your immediate circle to give you a more balanced perspective on the world. And you can most certainly learn to see your communication efforts not as a way to show off, but as a way to bring meaning to the people who need your expertise. Be proactive—talk to your colleagues in sales and marketing about your communication style.

If you're an executive or communications pro working with a technically minded individual fitting one or more of the above points—can you figure out a way to help that person overcome these challenges? Effective managers help employees identify shortcomings and work with them to find solutions. You can give them the time to focus on audience needs when putting together presentations. You can *gently* alert them to their myopia and suggest ways to broaden their worldview. And you can work with them directly to help them see how their frame of reference impacts their outreach efforts. Be proactive, but understanding.

7

Learning About Your Audience

Audience research, says Jay Labov, senior advisor for education and communication at the National Academy of Sciences, is critical in helping scientists shape important outreach strategies. The first experiment in using this research came as a team of scientists was developing a publication on the often-thorny subject of evolution. "Evolutionary biologists are fascinated with Darwin's finches," said Labov. "The American public . . . not so much." When asked about Darwin's finches, those famous Galapagos Islands birds that played such an important role in the inception of Darwin's theory of natural selection, polling subjects "just didn't care about the little brown birds."

The Washington, DC–based nonprofit found it highly beneficial to use focus groups, telephone surveys, and targeted interviews to help them, according to Labov, "find out what people want to know about science and the science of evolution more specifically, not just what scientists think people ought to know." The research helped members of the authoring committee and Academy staff see a long-term communication challenge in a new light.

The Academy was concerned by polls showing skepticism—or complete lack of acceptance—of evolution. Some critics of evolution believe supernatural explanations should also be included as part of a definition of science. These individuals assert that features of the universe and all living things in the universe are explained by an intelligent cause and not from only natural processes. These beliefs are at odds with the Academy and most mainstream religious organizations, both of which promote evidence-based scientific theory to answer questions about the diversity of life.

In 2008 the National Academy of Sciences along with the Institute of Medicine jointly authored and published the third edition of *Science, Evolution, and Creationism.* The third in a series of books on this topic, it was influenced by audience research conducted by a professional audience research organization that worked closely with Labov and his colleagues. This booklet sought to help people better understand evolution's underlying principles and role as an integral component of scientific research.[3] Labov explained that there are "a lot of people sitting on the fence" when it comes to the debate about evolution. The large group of undecideds was the target for the newest edition of their book. The Academy wanted to reach people with key messages to offer a fresh perspective on an age-old debate. With an effective use of audience research they were able to learn more about their audiences and what specifically would cause them to respond favorably to scientific information about evolution.

The first two editions of *Science, Evolution, and Creationism* included discussion on Darwin's finches. In the third edition, which followed new audience insights, the Academy changed the discussion.

What did excite the Academy's focus groups? Research revealed that people were more intrigued about the evolution of cetaceans—whales, dolphins, and porpoises. Scientists had discovered from fossil and molecular evidence that a succession of organisms moved from land to sea about 50 million years ago. The focus groups were intrigued—they wanted to know more about how cetaceans lost their hind limbs and developed more streamlined bodies and became the ocean mammals they are today.[4] Consequently, the committee that authored the book was able to use findings like this to produce a booklet with different approaches that more closely aligned with the interests of intended audiences.

Labov says they got a lot more out of the survey than what's described in the previous example. Doing the research helped them get into the minds of an audience that had perplexed them for so long. After years of assuming they understood disconnects between some Americans and the teaching of evolution, audience research enabled Labov and his colleagues to see the controversy of this issue with new eyes. That finding fueled significant changes in the development of their book and reshaped a critical argument. And that's really the whole point of knowing thy audience.

There are many ways to go about learning about your audience, from using free online tools to hiring a professional market research firm—with other options in between. Our discussion here focuses on the importance of audience research with a few recommendations to get you started.

Taking some time to think about your audience is a necessary practice no matter how straightforward the task, no matter how small the audience. Research is the foundation of good communication; you simply can't build an effective campaign—or write an email—without fully understanding who's on the receiving end.

Audience Research:
Getting Answers from the Source

Audience research can help us answer all kinds of important questions:

▷ What issues related to our subject evoke emotion from our audience?

▷ What media (television ads, in-person appearances, video clips, blogs) are most appealing to them?

▷ How much detailed information is appropriate?

▷ Who should be the primary spokesperson to deliver the message—an executive, a paid professional, a computer agent, or other?

▷ What topics should you avoid? What should you stress?

▷ What are the hot buttons? What will cause the audience to care about your topic?

With the answers to important questions like these, you'll be in a far better position to develop content that responds to your audience in a more customized manner.

BUILDING AWARENESS:
SMALL TO MID-SIZED AUDIENCES

The corporate world relies heavily on professional market research efforts to make decisions about developing and marketing products and services. You too may consider this option if you're working on a large or especially important project. Telephone surveys, interviews, and focus groups help us find out what consumers want whether it's in electronics or fashion or healthcare. Corporations spend big money to understand their markets. To them, market research is just another cost of doing business. They need to constantly have their finger on their audience's pulse. You as the communicator can benefit by doing the same with audience research.

What can you learn about your audience if you have a research company helping you out? Sometimes you are not sure what you are looking for or need an objective opinion. Professionals with survey design experience can help you decide what types of questions to ask and how to phrase those questions. Results generated from good audience research can be eye opening—or sometimes they just confirm what you expected. If you have a significant communication challenge—research can provide a window into your audience's mind that can be illuminating.

Unfortunately, audience research studies can cost enough money to put this tool out of reach for many organizations. But there are less expensive options if you are willing to be flexible. For a few thousand dollars you can get a market research company to tack on a few questions onto *omnibus survey*—an existing survey they're already conducting. You can get some of the data you need at a fraction of the cost.

Big-time communication efforts can warrant professional audience research costing in the tens to hundreds of thousands of dollars, but getting to know your audience usually doesn't require such extravagance. You can probably get by using lower budget, or even free techniques. Audience awareness can be easy—and sometimes takes only a few minutes—the important thing is that you take the time to focus on whom you're communicating to and figuring out what they need to get from you as the communicator.

Gathering information about your audience is easier today than ever before. Sometimes the answers to all you need to know about your audience—their interests, levels of education, or technical capabilities—is right at your fingertips. The Internet is an incredible tool to research audiences and will probably be your first stop as an audience investigator. The Web provides abundant information—professional and personal—about people. You can learn about their technical expe-rience or their academic achievements in seconds. Maybe they've writ-ten scholarly articles or blogs that could provide insight. Become a detective and find out what's relevant to your needs.

Social media is a relatively recent but especially useful tool to research audiences. Communicators like tools such as Facebook, Twit-ter, LinkedIn, and more because they *start a conversation* with audi-ences and engage them, unlike traditional single-directional media. Creating dialogue between parties leads to collecting information about individuals. We're just beginning to see how social media is unfolding as a research tool; we may not know exactly what the future holds in this area, but greater awareness of audience preferences is a near certainty. What we do know now is that its interactive nature offers intelligence gatherers and marketers a gold mine of information. Many of us may not be comfortable with the privacy issues these plat-forms present, but it's hard to overlook how social media can help us generate audience awareness.

If you're tasked with a bigger assignment with an audience of unknowns, you'll have to work a bit harder. I learned an easy approach to conduct audience research while working as a conference producer. It wasn't my job to be a specialist in any specific field (hence my lack of background in telecommunications). Instead, my task was to find out what topics business people wanted to learn more about so we could develop a targeted product for them. Solid audience research always proved to be the key to any conference's success. The approach was traditional, but it was effective.

It worked like this: I was assigned to research a specific industry or a current issue we believed important. I'd call insiders—executives and consultants—and talk to them about their most pressing con-cerns. I'd ask questions like: Are new regulations going to impact your business? Is there a new application for your product? Or does new technology impact your bottom line? After about three-dozen fifteen-minute interviews I'd usually have enough information about the mar-ket to determine if there was sufficient interest to produce a conference on the proposed topic. This formula worked surprisingly well. My calls weren't scientific (statisticians would probably be horrified by this approach), but my calls provided an adequate survey for my needs. If I read my market correctly, the chances for a profitable event increased significantly. In a week's time I could collect enough information about a potential audience to design an entire event.

This *free* audience research tool is something I still rely on today, though, admittedly, more of my research is likely to be done through social media and with fewer phone calls. Investing a few hours or days to discuss market trends or new developments with the right people can give you a beneficial perspective on audience development. You can find out if the topic you planned on presenting or writing about is already passé or too technical for audience members. You can learn what changes to make to adjust the focus of your presentation or paper. In short—you can prevent a train wreck from happening. Armed with the right information about your target audience, you can deliver highly focused content in your communication product.

8

Addressing Multiple Audiences

A rcheologists Dennis Stanford and Bruce Bradley argue that North America's first inhabitants came from Iberia . . . not Siberia. Around 21,000 years ago some very brave—and possibly very hungry—individuals crossed the North Atlantic by boat, surviving on marine animals and birds along the way, arriving at what's now the mid-Atlantic United States.[5] This theory throws everything we've been taught about the identities of the first Americans into the trash— it's a complete reversal of the Bering Strait model we all grew up learning.

Like anyone putting forth a new academic theory, Stanford and Bradley were expected to write a formal monograph to present their theories to their peers. When academics drop a bombshell of a theory like this—one challenging long established beliefs—they need to provide a thorough analysis to their community arguing many points of their discussion backed by hard data. The final product is often an extensive tome likely to be read by a handful of like-minded experts. A rigorous and time-consuming process, it's not uncommon for scholars to labor for years writing a book that'll be read by a very small audience—most academic books sell under a thousand copies. That's a lot of work for a small return.

Stanford, whom I dog-walk with regularly, is the kind of guy who wants to get his research into the hands of the people. When he and Bradley started writing *Across Atlantic Ice: The Origin of America's Clovis Culture,* they wondered if they could publish a book to satisfy scrutinizing scholars but also reach a broader audience with their exciting theory. Looking a bit like Grizzly Adams and exuding an aura of adventure like Indiana Jones, Stanford is a man of deep character who's passionate about his work. He wanted to share his bold new theory with everyone, not just a few peers.

The archeologists knew a secondary market existed—the *archeology/anthropology enthusiasts.* When I met up with Stanford at his office in the Smithsonian Institution's Museum of Natural History, he said he knew he was in for a challenge when he and Bradley decided they wanted to present their theory to both audiences: "We'd have to change scientific writing and eliminate a lot of the jargon to make the book more readable. We'd have to reduce the data so anyone could look at the data and charts and understand them." Stanford expected trouble down the road; making it more readable for the enthusiasts would make it less scientific for the academics. Could broadening the book's appeal alienate the all-important scholars? If the scholars rejected the book, Stanford and Bradley's theory could've suffered a grave defeat.

The trick was to find the perfect balance between scientific and popular writing styles and determine how much data they needed to present to satisfy the academics without boring the enthusiasts. This theory is more difficult than you may realize—to put forth a theory on this topic, Stanford and Bradley had to do research in the fields of archeology, paleoclimatology, oceanography, geology, and human biology—then explain it all in their book.

Making *Across Atlantic Ice* accessible to broader audiences meant more than cutting information to make it less overwhelming—it also meant adding a chapter to help give novices background information needed to understand the archeologists' process. Following the introduction, their first chapter is a primer on "flaked stone technology"— the stone artifacts that give us important details about our distant human heritage. Stanford and Bradley didn't intend this primer to be comprehensive, but culling the amount of data, writing the book in a more approachable style, and including a primer helped bring readers up to speed on technology and key principles used to understand how ancient tools helped to unlock the mysteries of the first Americans.

Stanford and Bradley breathed a sigh of relief a couple of months after *Across Atlantic Ice* was released. *The Journal of Field Archaeology, Prehistoric American*, and *American Archaeology* all gave favorable reviews. And book sales? Several thousand copies of *Across Atlantic Ice* sold within the first couple of months of being published . . . far more than anticipated.

Stanford and Bradley's approach was a lot of work. Their efforts were intensified by their decision to speak to two audiences instead of one. For your purposes, a one-size-fits-all approach may not always be an effective plan. If you want to produce a singular product designed to address disparate audiences—people with varied levels of experience in myriad subjects—be careful. It may seem easier to produce just one communication product for everyone, but it may not reach those varied audiences as effectively as you'd like.

Outreach efforts targeting one group of like-minded individuals are often easier than efforts that need to appeal to individuals with varied interests and abilities. With a single audience you can focus your efforts narrowly—providing just the right amount of information in a manner suited for that group. But once you add a second audience or more to the mix, your job becomes much more challenging.

As you start to write a document or plan a presentation, you need to use what you learned about your audience in order to deliver a communication product that's targeted specifically to them. This is why *knowing thy audience* is an important step. If you communicate complicated topics to multiple groups—whether they're venture capitalists, decision makers, academics, or subject enthusiasts—your interests will be best served if you speak to them directly and not as an anonymous entity.

Carefully consider the needs of all audiences when planning your communication strategy. Understand their educational and professional backgrounds. Determine how disparate the groups are—and to what extent their needs overlap.

THE MULTIPLE COMMUNICATION PRODUCT ROUTE

Often enough it makes sense to produce more than one communication product when you're talking to more than one audience. Cornell University science and technology professor Kathleen Vogel understands the importance of addressing multiple distinct audiences through separate communication vehicles. Her specialization—the production of knowledge on technical security policy—requires her to interact with two elite audiences: her academic colleagues and her defense and policy colleagues in Washington, DC. Both of these groups would be considered contemporaries, yet both require different information from her. Vogel faces a challenge that you're likely to encounter as a communicator—how to package your content for multiple audiences.

Examining how intelligence analysts produce knowledge about biological weapons threats—which is what Vogel does—is serious business. Learning about substances capable of killing dozens or even millions of people is a twenty-first-century imperative for governments. One group Vogel addresses, the policy and defense audience, is pragmatic about what they want from her. They're interested in how her academic framework can help them improve threat assessments. Vogel is to them both auditor and consultant—she pours over case studies provided by the U.S. government on suspected rogue states and criminal groups believed to be producing bioweapons. She collects data, analyzes it, then communicates her observations to the defense and policy communities so they can improve their ability to collect relevant information.

Vogel's efforts pay off for her government audiences: She often finds blind spots in the intelligence process and helps them understand weaknesses in their intelligence gathering. But Washington's defense elite isn't Vogel's only audience. As an academic at a major university, Vogel is required to share her research with her immediate professional peers. Academics, however, don't require the same information as the government. They're largely interested in how Vogel's work contributes to existing theory or concepts in academic literature—sharply different from the observations she provides the defense community.

For Vogel, creating two separate communication products is the most efficient approach to get the right information to her distinct audiences. She provides each group with the relevant information in a format that meets their expectations. Although it's more effort to generate different products, rather than employ a one-size-fits-all approach, the investment in time to develop an academic article and a more tactical presentation are clearly necessary to meet her professional requirements. Likewise, you'll probably find it's beneficial for you to communicate with different audiences by creating different products for each group. Effective communication products need to be targeted—multiple communication products help you achieve that.

CHAPTER

9

Researching Cultural Issues

Food, says former National Public Radio and BBC Radio host Rebecca Roberts, helps her explain scientific and technical subjects to her audiences. Food is something with which we all have first-hand experience and something we don't have to think about too deeply. The various textures, tastes, aromas, and looks of food offer an array of sensory experiences for all of us. Food can be bland, like a slice of processed white bread, or spicy, like a pungent curry. Whole grains can remind us of gritty sandpaper, while whipped cream can make us dream of fluffy clouds. Food is a great way to connect with people because we instantly recognize qualities we share as a culture through our culinary experiences.

Roberts says that references to food help her audience visualize scientific breakthroughs and novel engineering accomplishments. On radio she can't show photos, illustrations, or videos. She relies solely on language and sound to communicate whatever topic she is explaining. Roberts became, as she puts it, "a big fan of food analogies" while working as a science and technology reporter for BBC's *The World*: "My audience was educated but not necessarily knowledgeable in the areas of science and technology. I had to find ways to create a mental image that listeners could latch on to."

Roberts leans heavily on references to food because of the endless descriptive possibilities food provides. And within the realm of food, condiments are her favorite sub-category. For example, if Roberts wants to talk about a substance being sticky, she can make a natural connection to maple syrup. The mental image of maple syrup helps most North Americans viscerally and immediately understand the sticky quality of the substance Roberts is describing. In a flash she has succeeded in giving her audience an image they can grasp.

Of course, her approach only works when there is a common understanding or a shared experience of the world. It can become tricky across cultures. While maple syrup may work well for listeners tuning into Roberts's program in countries where people eat pancakes and waffles, maple syrup might not be a particularly good basis of comparison if she were speaking to an audience in rural China. The Canadians have tried to create a market for maple syrup in China, but from 2001 to 2008, Canada exported less than 40,000 liters of the sticky stuff to that country. Most Chinese, it's safe to say, have had little experience with the product and probably couldn't relate personally to a description dependent on maple syrup for understanding how sticky something is. Maple syrup is not going to work in China. A great image or analogy in North America could become a big mistake elsewhere.

Research is essential to understand your audience's level of cultural awareness. The Internet has made the world a smaller place by making it easier for people to connect. This is great—but it also means we need to consider that not everyone who will view our web pages or see our videos will comprehend certain references. There are cultural traits we need to think about if our audience comes from a different part of the country or different country altogether. In the digital age, communicators need to be more sensitive to the fact that their audiences may approach their content from a completely different viewpoint.

Look for Shared Experiences with Your Audience

Some experiences are universal and others are local. Consider this list of categories:

▷ **THE HUMAN EXPERIENCE.** There are some experiences that all 7 billion people living on Planet Earth share. Bodily functions are something that all of us can understand, for better or for worse. Likewise, we all understand the daily rising and setting of the sun, the passing of a year, and the need to eat.

▷ **A SLICE OF LIFE.** Recognizing products in a supermarket and the frustrations of highway traffic are among the situations that we might all encounter on any given day. Some of these experiences can be culturally based but still appeal to a general population.

▷ **POPULAR CULTURE.** Audiences readily grasp concepts when they are compared to television shows or movies, for example. But make sure that your audience is familiar with the base comparison. You can't necessarily expect someone living in Mumbai to grasp an analogy based on the popular American situational comedy *Modern Family*, any more than you could expect someone in New York to connect with a comparison from India's longest-running television series, *C.I.D.*

▷ SPORTS. Many audiences respond well to sports references. Most of the world is crazy about soccer—except in the United States, where fans are more obsessed with American football.

▷ HISTORY. Historical references work well because they put new concepts into a natural framework. Just be mindful that you will need to save more obscure historical references for better-informed audiences.

Effective communications often speak directly to target audiences. Referring to experiences that they know and love will help you endear yourself to them. There's a tradeoff when writing or talking about something that's localized. You draw one audience in, but run the risk of shutting others out.

Finding out what works in one culture and not in another takes research as well as logic. Whether you are trying to reach people in Albania or Alabama, it's up to you, the content developer, to have a sense of what your audience can appreciate or just tolerate. Use the Internet to learn about places and people that may be foreign to you. The more aware you are about another culture, the less likely you are to alienate them with references they do not understand.

III

Know Thy Subject

Writer James Reston Jr. believes you should know your topic thoroughly, but also believes you should use your knowledge purposefully. When Australian talk show personality David Frost hired him in 1976 to investigate President Nixon's involvement in the Watergate scandal for a series of television interviews, Reston knew learning every detail about the affair would be essential to succeed. The Frost/Nixon interviews, as they became known, proved to the American people that their former president had participated in the cover-up of the break-in at the Democratic National Committee headquarters in the Watergate complex. The climax of the interviews was an admission of the cover-up by Nixon, which Reston says would not have been likely if he hadn't prepared Frost thoroughly for the epic showdown.

"Frost had to achieve the same level of knowledge as the adversary so that he [Nixon] couldn't be patronizing and say you don't understand this, you don't understand that," Reston explained. "His mastery had to be so total that he not only asked the right questions with the right tone, but beyond that be quicker with reposts when Nixon came back with substandard answers."

If you saw the 2008 film *Frost/Nixon*, you know that Reston, portrayed by actor Sam Rockwell, and Reston's colleague, Bob Zelnick, portrayed by Oliver Platt, were challenged by Frost's initial lack of commitment to properly prepare for the series of interviews. Reston, who says Frost was "distracted and distractible" during the weeks leading up to the tapings, notes that both he and Zelnick faced a difficult task in "boiling down immensely complicated material [about Nixon's presidency] so that people could understand it." Frost was in show business . . . and wanted Reston and Zelnick to "translate all of this information into an interrogation strategy." But Frost wasn't too keen at the onset of doing much of the hard work to gain mastery of the topics himself.

In order for Frost to drive Nixon to a confession, it was Frost himself who had to become completely immersed in the details of the Nixon presidency. This didn't come until four days before the final interview—when Frost made the commitment to learn everything he could in the remaining time about the subject of the final interview—the Watergate break-in. Frost rebounded from three disastrous interviews and caught the former president off guard with his confidence and subject knowledge. He then injected a new piece of information, a damaging tape recording discovered by Reston about White House henchman Charles Colson's illicit activities. This new evidence, coupled with Frost's thorough understanding of the subject, stumped Nixon. The final interview ended with Frost as the clear winner.

You need mastery of your subject. While Reston and Zelnick were available to help guide Frost, the television talk show host was only able to triumph as a skilled interviewer and inquisitor once he immersed himself fully in the facts. He studied hard and learned his material thoroughly, but he doled out his newfound knowledge carefully—not spitting out everything he studied all at once. Holding back on information—and knowing when to masterfully insert your expertise—is communications excellence. Develop a thorough understanding of your subject before trying to explain it others . . . or nail someone in an interview.

In the words of the highly quotable Albert Einstein, "If you can't explain it simply, you don't understand it well enough." Thank you, Albert! This is an important point for communicators—especially for corporate trainers and professional communicators responsible for informing others on topics that are not within their area of expertise. There's a lot of knowledge we need to amass before we can take on the challenge of explaining complicated material with confidence. Too often, in our daily rush, we don't have the time or make the effort to learn all we should about new subject matter. That can come back to haunt us.

When communicators aren't sufficiently educated on the topic they need to explain, bad things can happen. The worst-case scenario is the delivery of misinformation—false statements that can lead people astray. If you're a public relations professional working for a nuclear power plant, for example, it could be problematic if you're not sufficiently schooled in the science and technology of your reactor and a crisis occurs. You may find yourself in a nuclear meltdown of your own if you're caught with insufficient project knowledge. From the worlds of finance, healthcare, science, and more—there are an unimaginable number of unpleasant situations that have occurred when communicators may have been a bit too leisurely when it came to studying their issues.

Failure to learn your topic inside-and-out can easily ruin your outreach effort. You can tell when a presenter is not fully confident in his material. You can see in his body language—how he hides behind a podium or twitches—there's a lack of uncertainty or ill ease. You probably pick up on this and subconsciously decide to mentally check out of the presentation. Maybe he's working directly from a training manual and is providing correct, useful information—but that doesn't matter; the audience has already tuned out.

Subject experts can be nervous working with writers or public relations advisors because they fear their meaty work will be reduced to superficial banter. Many of them have reason to be concerned. In the spirit of making specialized material accessible, some communicators go overboard and eliminate the essence of the subject. I marvel at television news programs that reduce subjects to a couple of trivial bullet points. They can take a topic like "storm preparedness" and tell you to stock up on water, bread, and toilet paper as if that's a revelation. Submitting a "fluff piece" to clients or giving a broad overview that glosses over important content can be just as bad.

10

If You Are Not a Subject Expert . . .

I was once assigned to help a group of NASA engineers to put together a document describing how the purchase of new equipment would make networking at NASA more efficient. My client set up a meeting for me with the engineers without explaining to them who I was and what my function would be. I got there and could immediately read on their faces: "Who's this guy?"

My first task had to be to establish my credibility. I told them that it's true I'm not a networking expert, but I am experienced in writing for engineers just like them. I listed the other NASA assignments I had worked on to assure them I wasn't just a public relations fluff who would turn their serious project content into superficial banter. I could see the expressions on their faces soften as I assured them of my skills and willingness to work with them as project partners.

With all I have to say about the importance of knowing thy subject, you may be surprised to learn that I don't have a formal background in science, technology, law, financial services, or just about any
other subject—other than communications that I've been hired to
communicate. A CIO client once told me he wanted to work with me
because he knows I approach each subject without bias. That's a good
thing. He believed that if I had preconceived ideas about a subject,
then I wouldn't approach an assignment with an open mind. For him,
my lack of subject-specific knowledge is an asset because I can explain
complicated subjects to nonspecialists in everyday language. A little
knowledge can be dangerous—the failure to recognize something as
too technical for nonspecialist audiences can creep into your writing
without you realizing it.

Although I've made a career out of writing about subjects in which
I have no formal training, I've always done my best to learn as much
about my topic as I could before sitting down to write. Typically, the
first step is an input session, ideally between a technical expert or
experts and me. They provide specific information and I take notes.
When it's a meeting specifically related to my preparation of a communication product, I am free to ask as many questions as I can, and I
do.[1] Sometimes, however, I am asked to sit in on meetings where
everyone in the room but me is an experienced subject pro and I don't
have the opportunity to ask for explanation; these meetings can be
excruciating. The best I can do is to take good notes and find a friendly
face in the crowd and ask for help later as I try to piece it all together.

In either scenario, content subject experts can provide information that goes over my head. They use jargon, acronyms, and facts
assuming knowledge of prerequisite subjects. The content is often
intimidating. I try not to worry if I don't understand everything
immediately. I use an electronic pen that records conversations as I
am writing notes. When I get back to the office, I play back the
recording by tapping the pen tip on a word in my notes and it goes
directly to the point in the discussion to which I want to listen.[2] This
is more efficient than a standard tape recorder. At this point I'll also

initiate online work to Google terms I don't understand or to gather background information. Wikipedia is often a good source for background, but I'm careful to check footnotes and confirm anything I learn from that site.

Feedback plays an essential role as I cobble together an understanding of what needs to be communicated. I'll take a stab at drafting content and ask for comments from the specialists. I'll be persistent in tracking them down because the people I'm trying to help are inevitably too busy to talk to me. I offer them flexibility in carving out time to meet and will stay on top of them until the job is done. I'll also ask if they can direct me to someone on their staff who can help me with background. Writing about complicated topics for other people needs to be a process—there must be a back-and-forth conversation between specialist and writer. If it's truly complicated, you're not likely to gain mastery after a single input session. The specialist should be advised of his or her role and the time commitment/process up front.

Guidelines for Engaging with Specialists

Consider these steps before engaging with specialists on an assignment:

1. The first few minutes you spend with subject matter experts is critical. Introduce yourself as a communication expert who can help them look good. Establish your credibility upfront. Let them know you respect their work . . . make sure they respect yours!

2. Advise them of the importance of the communication effort. Tell them nonspecialists need to understand their work if they are to get more funding, regulatory approval, or meet another goal. You're there to work with them, not take over.

3. Be transparent. Don't lie about experience you don't have. Explain that your lack of expertise in their topic gives you a fresh pair of eyes to see their subject with clarity. You have no biases to bring to the assignment. But let them know that you have experience helping clients explain equally complicated material.

4. Let them know what you expect of them. They should be patient when explaining complicated topics and must offer you availability for review.

5. Take good notes and record conversations if allowed.

6. If you don't understand an important point early in the conversation, stop them and ask them to explain it again. Be assertive.

7. When you get back to your office, review and write up your notes and fill in the blanks with your recording device.

8. Go online and see what information you can find to fill in some of the blanks your colleagues didn't tell you, but don't use that content in your end product unless you have the experts' approval.

9. Write drafts and share them with content experts. Then rewrite as needed until you get it right.

Your goal is to distill content to a point where it's manageable for nonspecialists to comprehend—but just because you'll be writing fewer words does not mean you can be a slacker when it comes to doing research. Effective communicators know details . . . they just choose to use them strategically.

CHAPTER
11

Advice for Content Experts

This chapter speaks to engineers, scientists, and other smart folks who may be brilliant at what they do but are challenged in getting nonspecialists informed, let alone excited, about a technical subject. Bad writing or ineffective speaking can kill your project before it gets off the launch pad. If you can't articulate your message in a way that your audience can comprehend, you can't expect them to share your enthusiasm—let alone write a check. Too many technically minded folks don't get it that their brilliance can be overlooked if it's not understood.

If this describes you—please take action before an important opportunity slips away. Improving your writing skills is a noble pursuit if you're not especially adept in this area, but keep in mind that effective writing isn't something you're likely to learn overnight. It takes years of education, followed by even more years of practice. And remember also that some people are just naturally inclined to be good writers but might not have your technical skills. Public speaking can be improved with good direction, but you still have to know how to package your information in a way that's meaningful for your audience.

This book will help you cross certain hurdles. But if you're truly struggling in your efforts to decomplicate content, you may need professional help. Working with a professional communicator can help you reach new heights faster than anticipated. If you work for a large institution there may be preapproved assistance available. Look into these valuable options. If you're with a smaller organization or work independently, there are many qualified writer/editors looking for pick-up assignments. You'll still need your copy of *Supercommunicators*, however, because as the content expert you need to provide your communicator with direction. The greater awareness you have of the communication process and the more involved you are, the better the end product will be.

Guidelines for Working with Writers

Working with a communicator isn't always easy for subject experts. Here are a few tips if you are new to this idea:

▷   Make sure your writer is qualified. Writers should have experience working on the kind of document or product with which you need help. They don't need to be a subject expert if your assignment is to communicate to nonspecialists. Technical writers (writers with technical background) are preferred when you need to explain a highly technical subject to other specialists.

▷   Give writers a chance—cooperate with them. View them as an ally who can help make your vision a reality ... not an obstruction keeping you from the lab, the office, or a meeting.

▷   Offer writers background information so they can educate themselves on information relevant to your subject. If you're too busy, refer them to other colleagues who can fill them in as needed.

▷   Make time for them. If the project is important, you will find time in your schedule to meet with your writer in person, by phone, or by Skype.

▷   Give regular, constructive feedback. Be patient. Tell a writer to do it over if it's not acceptable.

You may be able to find someone affiliated with a local university or an individual who is employed full-time but in search of extra income to help alleviate your editorial woes. You can also find countless writers/editors willing to help you for a small fee from any number of online bulletin boards. Top-of-the-line professional writers can charge over $100 an hour for their time, but there are many competent guns for hire for under $50 an hour—often cheaper if outsourced online. On some websites you can have writers bid to do work for you based on a description you provide. Just make sure your hired hand has sufficient experience and good credentials.

PART IV

Simplicity and Clarity

Supercommunicators know the difference between simplicity and clarity. By definition, *simplicity* means being easy to understand or do, or, in the words of Merriam-Webster, "the state of being simple, uncomplicated or uncompounded."[1] *Clarity,* however, is defined as "clearness or lucidity as to perception or understanding."[2] Our job as communicators is to make content more meaningful and understandable for our audiences. This can mean making ideas simpler at times, but at other times it may require us to strive for clarification.

HOMAGE TO SIMPLICITY

I asked Vinay Rai, an Indian entrepreneur on the Forbes Global 200 list in 1999, how he introduced several innovations to the Indian marketplace. After earning a master's degree in engineering at the Massachusetts Institute of Technology, Rai returned to his native country to play a pivotal role in driving the adoption of technologies such as the transistor and the cell phone. I assumed the entrepreneur had faced many communication obstacles in his career. For people to embrace new products, they first have to comprehend them, but the under-stated Rai said he never thought too hard about explaining them. "Just make things as easy as you can for others to understand," he told me. Not fully satisfied with his response, I asked him, "How did you explain the concept of cell phones to a highly rural audience with no familiarity with that technology?" He replied, "I told them: This is your phone . . . it just walks around with you."

Rai didn't talk to farmers about frequencies, cell clusters, and spectrum efficiency when explaining mobile telephony—why over-complicate the situation? His simple, one-line description was all that was needed to get the job done. In the span of a decade, the number of cell phones in India exploded from 6.5 million to over 900 million. Maybe Rai is onto something?

By giving our audience more detail, using bigger words, and creat-ing grander sentences, some think we'll be more successful in getting them to understand our complicated topic. Effective communication is about reaching your audience and getting them to understand your point. Don't complicate when you can simplify.

Simplification is nothing new. Classic American writer Henry David Thoreau quipped about our lives being "frittered away by detail" in his writings from Walden Pond. He urged us to "simplify, sim-plify."[3] He wrote these words in the early nineteenth century, a time when the United States was undergoing a transformation that would make permanent changes to our society.

Railroads were expanding and America was rapidly connecting to the world economy when Thoreau wrote *Walden*. This was an unwel-come disruption to many farmers and small-town residents scared of the evils the whistling iron horse would bring. An Ohio school board member warned, "If God had designed that His intelligent creatures should travel at the frightful speed of 15 miles an hour by steam he would have foretold it through His holy prophets. It is a device of

Satan to lead immortal souls down to Hell."[4] Farmers were learning that their simple way of life was forever changing. The roots of the simplicity movement are rooted in this first big push to industrialization and globalization. Today many of us share similar sentiments with the nineteenth-century agrarians.

People resist change, especially if it takes them out of their comfort zone. The unknown is scary. In the twenty-first century we have plenty of our own transformations to deal with as nanotechnology, synthetic biology, artificial intelligence, biotechnology, and other innovative forces are set to alter our lives. Uninformed citizens will rise up once again afraid of devils and demons. Thoreau's wisdom will hold true. We need to simplify. People need to understand the big changes coming our way. The best way for us to reach them is by delivering meaningful, understandable information. Our job as communicators is to provide them with truth about transformative changes in a way they can understand.

But one factor Thoreau didn't have to contend with two centuries ago was that communication was limited to writing and speaking. The arrival of digital communication is a wonderful disruption, but it does require us to delve deeper into the art of simplicity. The Internet compels us to streamline our ideas and shorten our discussions. Twitter teaches us to reduce communication to 140 characters instead of writing in volumes, compelling us to embrace brevity along with simplicity.

ODE TO CLARITY

Simplicity isn't everyone's friend. I find this true with engineers and scientists who argue that public relations *schlocks* like to distill their ideas to a point where they're no longer recognizable. That's not good. If we dumb down everything too much, we're left with nothing but superficial banter stripped of meaning. Simplicity can be a double-edged sword.

Effective communications help audiences see complicated topics more clearly. They reveal realities that have been obscured by veils of complexity. Use your presentation, graphic, or text to unravel the mystery. Help your audience see patterns they couldn't visualize on their own. Flag important points covered up by jargon or specialized language. Bring to the surface essential facts that may be lost in a block of extraneous detail.

Integrity matters. You never want to simplify anything to the point where you alter the meaning of your message. This is especially true in cases where audiences need specific information and key facts can't be eliminated. For example, if you were explaining new audit methodologies to a group of auditors, it would be disastrous if you glossed over details that are pertinent to their jobs. Following generally accepted auditing standards (GAAS) isn't a suggestion—it's an imperative for anyone working in that field. Trainers who work with auditors to comprehend new standards and requirements must be focused on making content more comprehensible without omitting crucial steps.

SIMPLICITY VS. CLARITY

Simplicity and clarity are similar in many ways, but different in other ways. The take-away here is that your job is to make content more accessible. Once again, it's essential to "know thy audience." Is your audience like the Indian farmers? They'll be able to get along without understanding the technology behind cellular communication. Or is your audience more like the auditors? They need to know about new standards in requirements or they won't be able to do their jobs.

When to simplify and when to clarify are judgment calls you the communicator need to make. The more you understand your audience and the better you understand your topic, the more likely you'll be able to know when to simplify and when to clarify.

12

Simplify Your Content

> "There is always a simple way to understand
> big ideas."   —IRA FLATOW

"There are some details that are important to some but may be beyond the understanding of me or other people," Ira Flatow, author and host of the popular NPR radio program *Science Friday,* explained to me. And there's nothing wrong with that. It's okay for individuals with varied backgrounds and interests to learn about new subjects at different levels of depth. "People love science," he says, but those seeking to educate us about science haven't done an especially good job of teaching us to appreciate it like we are taught to appreciate art. There aren't many opportunities for most of us to gain big picture awareness about advancements in science or technology—but

Science Friday is an exception. The program's 1.3 million global listeners tune in each week for a broadcast that piques their curiosity about a broad range of topics in science and technology.[5] Part of the broadcast's success, notes Flatow, is that they don't drill down so deeply into topics that their discussions become boring or too taxing to the majority of their listenership—intellectually curious people.

Flatow's commitment to make technical content easier for broader audiences extends to his books as well. *Present at the Future* is filled with great examples of challenging topics made easier to understand by avoiding minutiae and focusing on big picture ideas instead. He offers welcoming discussions on "difficult" subjects like cosmology and gray matter in physics that lead you to an "aha" point of understanding. You don't have to have a Ph.D. in engineering to comprehend his chapter on nanotechnology, for example. Flatow introduces this topic by explaining the origin of the term, offers a brief historical overview to put the subject in context, then continues to explain nanotechnology while presenting the benefits associated with this new field. He describes how nanotechnology can revolutionize electronics by shrinking a computer chip down to the size of a single molecule[6] or how bionanotechnology can be useful in medicine by helping doctors detect a virus in real time.[7] That's the kind of information enthusiasts want to know about. By omitting potentially tiresome discussion on the inner workings of nanotechnology, and focusing instead on its benefits, he is engaging his audience with meaningful information.

Flatow's advice to scientists and technologists is to go ahead and savor the beauty of the details you see in your subject, just don't think everyone else needs or wants to experience it at the same granular level. "If you look at a flower you see the beautiful petals, you see the gorgeous colors—it's just a beautiful thing of nature. But a scientist or someone interested in nature who studies the actual structure of the petals, the cells, the pigments, and the mathematical progression of the petals . . . they'll have a different joy of the flower than someone who enjoys it just for its natural beauty. You can see a whole different kind of structural beauty that makes it more fascinating."

Sometimes you have to leave out details. One of the reasons scientists, engineers, and other big idea generators don't always succeed in generating excitement about new discoveries or innovations is that they often bog down audiences with too much information. Give them too much detail and they'll miss seeing the big picture.

If you're a specialist discussing a complicated topic, you may feel compelled to share every glorious detail with the world. But please restrain yourself. Perhaps it's the sheer joy you get from doing your work or the thrill you've experienced by making a new discovery, but hold back. If you are one of the scientists, economists, lawyers, or other professionals lucky enough to be engaged in a project that you're passionate about . . . great. But remember, not everyone is going to be interested in the same level of detail you find exciting.

We humans are naturally programmed to seek out meaning before we're able to pick up on finer details. Introducing a key idea up front is essential before piling on additional points.[8] Make sure you give your audience context—give them a reason to care so they'll pay attention and become engaged. If you can't offer them a broad view of the topic you're discussing and understand the premise of your idea up front, there's really no reason for you to continue with the rest of your presentation. They're already lost! How much more meaningful would my meeting with the Chilean CTO have been if he gave me context before launching into a highly technical discussion?

Remember Dr. Fauci's "know thy audience" advice from Part II. The more you know about who's sitting before you or who's reading your report, the better your chances for reaching them with pertinent content. Audience awareness gives you the opportunity to think through what information will resonate with them. Equipped with a sense of their needs, you're more likely to develop content that helps you whittle away extraneous ideas and get to the core of your message.

THE WINNOWING PROCESS

Some information is relevant to some but not to others, and some information is not relevant to anyone. But deciding what content to include and what to trash requires serious thought. I can tell when another dog-walking friend, Adrianne Threatt, is in her "winnowing process" mode. Sometimes when I see her walking Amos and Jacob, two mixed-breed shepherds with fabulously plumed tails, at 6:45 in the morning, I feel like I can see the wheels turning in her head as she's processing information she learned the previous day. The former senior counsel on the Financial Services Democratic Staff in the United States House of Representatives played a critical role in writing the Dodd–Frank Wall Street Reform and Consumer Protection Act. She spent months buried under piles of documents before she could write a single sentence of the bill. Threatt immersed herself in an exhaustive study of all pertinent issues during her "deep analytic dive" only to follow that period up with an equally strenuous task of weeding out the minutiae.

And there she is—winnowing as she walks. That's the kind of intensity you should be aiming for when editing detailed content; your colleagues—and dog-walking friends—should be able to see the concentration in your face. Absorb as much data as you can and then let your brain go to work to sort it all out. Cull information and determine what to bring to the forefront and what to toss aside. Some information is important for some audiences but irrelevant to others. Think about what content to keep and for whom to keep it.

For some, like Threatt, this is a mental exercise. Others, however, may choose to commit their ideas to paper. Create a simple box chart in a Word document or an Excel spreadsheet with your target audiences in the left column and put key points in the right column. Populate the left side of your template with the different stakeholders who will need information from you. Who are they? For an IT project, for example, your stakeholders may include the governing board, CIO, deputy CIO, business management office, and systems administrators.

On the right side, type in bits of information that would be relevant to each of these groups. The CIO probably needs big-picture information, whereas the deputy CIO with more oversight responsibility will require more detail. The systems analysts are likely to require a much different set of points since their responsibilities are more hands-on. This simple template can make a difference in helping you clarify what messages are relevant to which audiences. If you want to impress associates with your new chart, call it a *stakeholder analysis template.*

It doesn't matter how you choose to cull information and assign key topics to audiences. What's important is that you have broken down what you thought of as a beastly topic with multiple arms and legs and shaped it into a more manageable pursuit. It's important that you learn as much as you can about the subject, but it's equally important that you reason through what's relevant in that heap of data to various audiences. You are better equipped to simplify content for others once you have simplified it for yourself.

13

But Don't Oversimplify

Early in my research I had the pleasure of interviewing Vint Cerf, one of the "fathers of the Internet."[9] I wanted to see how this legendary techie would explain his creation: TCP/IP technology or, in layman's terms, that which makes the Internet work.

Cerf offered me a line he borrowed from another brilliant innovator of the twentieth century, Albert Einstein. He looked me straight in the eye and told me that the key to communicating complicated topics is simplicity—but with a big caveat. "Everything should be made as simple as possible, but not simpler," he uttered.

What came next was a walk through the history of the Internet. Cerf proceeded to exemplify his lesson on "simplify, but don't oversimplify." He discussed early efforts to build the Internet by the U.S. government in the 1960s, then continued onto the 1970s when he started working with Bob Kahn at the U.S. Department of Defense Advanced Research Projects Agency (DARPA). It was there that Cerf and Kahn's team determined how the Internet data should get formatted, addressed, transmitted, routed, and received. He pushed onward to discuss the Internet's commercialization and his work at former telecommunications giant MCI. We talked about technology and policy issues as well. I was getting a crash course in the Internet from the master himself.

As he was talking, I was thinking, "How many times has he explained how the Internet works?" Google's Chief Internet Evangelist, Cerf has perfected his lesson over four decades. Practice certainly helps. By explaining his message over and over again he can gauge just how much complexity he can deliver without alienating people. Cerf knows he can't dumb down his explanation too much; what he wants to convey shouldn't be reduced to superficial banter.

DON'T INSULT YOUR AUDIENCE!

Some audiences try to comprehend some topics that may be challenging and brace themselves accordingly. They turn on their hyperfocus capabilities. They are willing to meet you halfway to try to comprehend the complicated. Don't oversimplify when your audience needs substantial content. Too often communicators are so concerned about scaring people off that they reduce their presentations and papers into meaningless fluff. This does no one any good. You may be trying to help your audience, but in actuality you may be accused of pandering to them. Assuming an audience doesn't have the capacity to learn something technical belittles them and makes you come across as arrogant. Show respect for your audience and don't insult them. Clarify complicated topics, but don't simplify meaningful information that's important for them to learn.

Knowing what material to include and what to leave out is critical to explaining anything. There are no hard and fast rules to follow regarding what should be presented to your audience and what should be tossed into the trash. Finding the right formula—the perfect balance of "simple enough, but not too simple" content—is an art form in itself.

Our discussion of simplicity is about removing barriers that might otherwise prevent audiences from gaining access to information. We put up fences in our communication efforts without realizing it. Some extraneous content here, too much jargon there . . . it all adds up to preventing access for nonspecialists. Striving for simplicity means cutting through all the noise to distill messages to their core; let's remove roadblocks that keep audiences from comprehension.

Don't Let "Information Smog" Bog You Down

How are we going to take a break from the "information smog"[10] we breathe every day? Paul Laudicina, the author of Beating the Global Odds, *suggests we "seek out tools and trends in the modern context that enhance simplicity, sustainability, and self-fulfillment. Avoid, eliminate, or minimize those that do not." The global chairman of consulting firm A.T. Kearney says we need to be clear about our strategic intent and then adopt the "products, processes, and systems that support that strategy."[11]*

CHAPTER

14

Focus on Clarity

In 2012 the U.S. Patent Trademark Office (USPTO) received 576,763 patent applications.[12] Former Patent Commissioner Bob Stoll tells me a significant number of these were returned to sender because of issues concerning "improper idiomatic English."[13] That is, the patent inspectors couldn't understand the submission. It could be a translation issue—many applicants are non-native English speakers—but too often the problem is that the technologies or products in review aren't properly explained. Inventors spend time, money, and effort building new ideas, but don't always invest the effort to deliver a clear explanation of them. Applicants must feel frustrated when their patents are delayed on account of poor communication. Patent delays are costly mistakes that can set your business back. It's even more painful when you realize these errors could have been avoided if a qualified writer spent just a few hours cleaning up your application.

Nothing kills good ideas like poorly written text. You could have found the cure for cancer or an alternative power source, but if you can't articulate your concept clearly and intelligibly, you're going to have a much harder time getting people to believe your claim. The same holds true for speaking; the fussier you make your presentation, the harder it will be for people to follow. There are lessons to be learned for presenters in this chapter, but our primary focus is on bringing clarity to your writing.

In the previous chapter we examined how right-sizing content for your audience is a critical factor in communicating complicated concepts. But just because you have the correct amount of targeted content doesn't mean you're finished. Your ideas must be molded into a product, like a document or web block, in a way that informs your audience with clarity and ease. You may have simplified your content significantly by leaving out extraneous details. Now your task is to put your ideas into words that will seamlessly deliver meaning to intended parties.

While most everyone knows how to write, many don't know how to write well. Your eighth grade teacher wasn't kidding when she tried to explain to you the importance of the inflections and syntax of language. Be mindful of bad grammar and other foibles—they can easily sour a reader's perception of your ideas. If you are prone to make grammatical mistakes, always make sure someone checks your work before it circulates. But even if your content is error free, your audience still might not be able to make any sense of your discussion.

In our rush to get more information quickly, we have less tolerance for roadblocks that prevent us from getting to the meat of the matter. "Don't slow me down with big vocabulary words," or "Don't use jargon that only geeks can understand," is the prevalent feeling among today's digital citizens. So while the rules of writing simply haven't changed, our expectation that content providers offer us clarity is higher. It is your responsibility to make sure that your text is as effortless as possible for your reader. This means removing any road-blocks that slow down a fluid exchange of ideas.

Critically look at your content. Are you using big words unnecessarily? Are your web pages filled with jargon? Are your sentences and paragraphs too long? All of these and other factors can bog down your reader. If you aren't sure your writing is sufficiently simple, check out a tool in Microsoft Word that helps you check up on the readability of your writing. Paul Smith, author of *Lead with a Story*, told me about this feature that calculates your Flesch-Kincaid Grade Level automatically. It's simple. Depending on the version of Word you're using, select "Check grammar with spelling." Click on "Options," then find and click on "Show readability statistics." After you run through the spell and grammar check, you'll see a pop-up that provides useful information about the complexity of your document. You can see what grade level you're writing at, as well as determine your Flesch-Kincaid Grade Level.

Many business people write at college level—somewhere between grades 12 and 15. That's too challenging for most audiences even if they are college graduates. You want to shoot for somewhere between grade level 8 and 10 on this scale when communicating to a professional audience. *The New York Times* and similar publications typically score in this range. Although many *Times* readers are capable of reading at a higher level, the *Times* knows that writing in a simple style will make their stories easier to understand. If you prefer to use the Flesch-Kincaid scale, you should aim for a score of higher than 60 percent. Neither of these scales measures the intelligence of your writing. They merely point out if your text is too complicated. Your ideas may be great, but the way you're explaining them is too fussy.

PART

V

Guidelines for Effective Communication

I was summoned to one of the Central Intelligence Agency's off-campus offices on a matter of national importance. Tim Kilbourn, Dean of the CIA's Sherman Kent School for Intelligence Analysis, wanted to question me about what I know about digital communication. His questions were fair, and I gave truthful answers, but then I turned the table on him and asked him a few questions of my own. "What does the CIA do to assure complicated subjects are communicated effectively?" I asked. That's when I uncovered the Agency's secret weapon: *The Analyst's Style Manual*, which lists the six rules for effective intelligence writing[1]:

1. **PUT YOUR MAIN IDEA UP FRONT.** Inform your readers right away about what's important and why.

2. **WRITE SHORT PARAGRAPHS.** Keep the reader's interest and

reduce the overload of information for the reader by writing short, well-developed paragraphs.

3. USE ACTIVE VOICE. Create mostly active sentences—avoid passive voice.

4. USE SHORT, CONVENTIONAL WORDS. Conventional, but precise, concrete words are best.

5. WRITE SHORT SENTENCES. Limit sentences to what you can say aloud in one breath.

6. BE CORRECT, CREDIBLE, AND COMPLETE. Make sure your work is as error free as possible.

The CIA is in the information business; analysts spend more time writing reports than conducting James Bond style espionage. Kilbourn says the Agency invests a lot of time in training new hires to write with precision. Simplifying content to its essence is a must for the CIA . . . and should be for anyone else attempting to communicate complicated material effectively.

The Analyst's Style Manual is available online for free. You may wish to use it, or seek out another manual more specific to your needs. Using style guides is a great way to improve your writing skills and bring consistency to your work. Take note that some companies and industries prefer certain style guides—publishers, for example, like *The Chicago Manual of Style,* whereas publications tend to use *The AP Style Manual.* You should check with people in your company or industry to find out if they have a preference or even have a style guide of their own.

I prefer using the word *guidelines* instead of *rules* when discussing writing. People like rules better because they're more certain, more black and white. If you follow rules, some argue, you won't go wrong as there is no gray area. But unless you're working on a highly technical document where precision is a mandate, you're going to have to get a bit messy and work through a number of subjective issues to effectively reach your audience.

If rules are what make writing a science, subjectivity is what makes it an art. Communicating complicated material to nonspecialists requires that you learn a delicate dance. You need to exemplify clarity while simultaneously keeping your audience engaged. These two ideas are often at odds with each other. Clarity suggests simplifying language, cutting down on extraneous thoughts and words and organizing ideas logically so your audience can grasp the concept more readily. That's all essential. The conundrum, however, is that following effective communication "rules" to a tee can be boring. When you're too orderly you can lose your audience to fatigue. If I followed the "don't use big words rule," for example, I would be in trouble already for using a big word like "conundrum." This is why I prefer "guidelines" to rules. Many effective communicators break rules all the time when it's necessary to the content.

15

Supercommunicator Basic Guidelines

LEAD WITH THE CONCLUSION

Think about the president of the United States reading through his early morning reports. His daily briefer from the CIA arrives and hands him a stack of reports intended to update him on political upheavals and other issues going on around the world. It would take him hours to read everything that's put before him from start to finish. He's likely to read the summary up front of one document, then continue onto the next. If he engages in an issue of particular importance in one document, he might decide to delve further. The president is getting the most essential information he needs, but is using his time effectively by not reading exhaustive tomes on topics that aren't especially important to him. This is why the first rule on the CIA's list tells you to "put your main idea up front."

In the not-too-distant past, we were taught to lead people into a discussion with our introduction. We would continue to build on our concept in the body of the document and then conclude with our main idea. With the exception of academic work, this practice is quickly becoming ancient history. Today, we're not sure our information-soaked audience will stick around long enough to get to the conclusion.

This approach is a more effective way of making sure the people you need to reach get your message. They may not read your entire document from start to finish like they would have in the old days, but at least you will have succeeded in getting your most critical ideas across. If your subject is of importance to your reader, then he or she will continue. The body of the document is becoming increasingly used to support claims made in the front part of documents.

Fewer people may be reading the bulk of your document, but that doesn't mean you can take short cuts. If you don't have the goods to back up the claims you make in your introduction, savvy readers will likely see through the veneer. It's just as important today to write a comprehensive document with supporting information as it was in the past.

The Internet is ideally suited to give people essential information up front along with the opportunity to dig deeper if they choose. You can tell users your main ideas up front and include links to text where they can access more information. Most websites you visit offer you this option. You scan the page until you see something that strikes your interest, then click to get to the topic that is most relevant to you. But as a content developer, be careful with links. I've seen many eager-to-please types put too many links into their text. When this happens, users can get distracted—and even worse, leave your website.

Some communication pieces, like this book, aren't suited to "leading with a conclusion." If I were writing a CIA report, a strategic plan for NASA, or any number of different types of documents for a client, I would do what I suggest above. But sometimes a communication opportunity doesn't lend itself so neatly to the "lead with your conclusion" approach. In these cases, I often choose the "lead with a story" plan. Storytelling warrants a chapter of its own. You can find that in Chapter 18.

USE BIG WORDS SPARINGLY

"He is a wonderful orator," my friend Clarice says of her preacher. Every Sunday she looks forward to his sermon. "He's so capable of engaging his congregation on a variety of topics," Clarice sings his praises. He's perfect, except for a tiny thing. Her highly educated preacher loves to use big words. One of his favorites is *theoria*. Greek for contemplation, *theoria* was picked up by Christians centuries ago to describe various forms of prayer and the process of coming to know God.[2] *Theoria* is a great word. It defines a specific idea succinctly; that's what good words do. The only problem is that most people in Clarice's parish, educated people but not theologians, don't know what it means. "When he first used the word, my first reaction was to think of a word that rhymed with theoria," noted Clarice. "Every week it jars me and I lose track of what he's saying because I am thinking of that word instead of concentrating on the sermon."

It's good to have a strong vocabulary. People with bigger vocabularies tend to do better professionally. But knowing when to toss around big words is a subjective call. Rusty Burke of the Johnson O'Connor Research Foundation says he is aware of the dictum that says you should stick to a sixth-grade vocabulary when writing for a broad audience. "Perhaps this is so," he notes, "but I think it's more important that one knows more than a sixth grader. The broader your vocabulary, the easier it will be for you to find the right words to communicate clearly with your intended audiences." So it is good to have a large and exact vocabulary, but that doesn't mean you have to throw every big word you know into your document or conversation.

Confused? The above sentence goes against what many of us have been taught. While research shows that people with strong vocabularies are more successful in business, we also know that people who use big words make lackluster communicators. This is another conundrum. You need good verbal scores on your SATs to get into a top-flight university; then, once there, your professors will encourage you integrate these elaborate words into your essays. But continue to use your impressive vocabulary in the workplace and you'll be in for a rude surprise. Elaborate words are ineffective if your audience is thinking more about your vocabulary than what you have to say. As Clarice discovered, big words can disrupt a homily—and that holds true for business communications as well.

In most cases you should use shorter, simpler words—unless, of course, you have a stylistic reason for using a bigger word. Don't let your strong vocabulary turn you into an out-of-touch elitist. Most audiences, other than academic elites, find elaborate words off-putting. Make sure you don't use them to impress or show off. People want easy, not imposing.

In Praise of "Plain and Ordinary"

John L. Beckley explains the big word guideline nicely in his classic book The Power of Little Words: *"Whenever you want something to be extremely clear, or something sounds stuffy or stilted, replace the longer, less common word with shorter, simpler expressions. Look for plain, ordinary conversational words that give an immediate, sharp impression."[3]*

COMBAT JARGON ABUSE

When you use jargon, special words, or expressions specific professions or groups use, you're creating a barrier between yourself and your audience. Like membership in a private club, you may feel warm and fuzzy if included, but if you're the person unable to get past the security desk, you may feel purposefully left out. Jargon makes people feel excluded. Communicating the complicated is about inclusivity, not exclusivity. Building a moat around your topic—segregating your ideas only to people who understand your private language—is one of the worst things you can do.

In most cases, people use jargon because that's what's comfortable to them. They probably aren't trying to exclude you, Mr. or Ms. Nonspecialist. But regardless of their intent, that's exactly what they're doing. Jargon is the native language of specialists who live in a bubble. They are unaware that not everyone has incorporated a particular word or expression into their vocabulary, and often they're just saying what comes naturally to them without thinking about how it sounds to others. If a lawyer uses the word *emoluments* several times a day when speaking with peers, she may neglect to remember that nonlawyers may not comprehend that term. She would be better off saying "a person's earnings" instead of that off-putting technical term, which sounds like a chemical used in embalming.

Most cases of jargon abuse aren't intended to be malicious, but *Financial Times* writer Jonathan Guthrie believes some communicators, especially marketers, use jargon purposely to mislead. He describes jargon as "a shrewd device to manipulate competitors, customers and colleagues."[4] Guthrie points to a response to a would-be Virgin Trains traveler inquiring why the company website neglected to display a particular route price. Virgin's response: "Moving forward, we, as Virgin Trains, are looking to take ownership of the flow in question to apply our pricing structure, thus resulting in this journey search appearing in the new category-matrix format."[5] Virgin earned a "Golden Bull" award for its use of jargon for this response because it purposely prevented a customer from understanding what it was talking about.

As is the case with "big words," the solution to combat jargon abuse is awareness. Are you using too many industry-specific terms when you communicate to people outside your circle? Have you and your colleagues developed your own special language no one else can understand? Review work you have shared with nonspecialist colleagues with a critical eye. Think about how they see your funny vocabulary. Or better yet, ask them to go over one of your papers and have them point out terms that befuddle them.

The solution to jargon abuse: replace jargon with words that real people use. Invite the outsiders into your club so they can more easily understand your topic and why it is important. In many situations, you can simply replace jargon with more commonly used words and terms. If, however, the insider term used by specialists so accurately describes what you're writing about that you feel you must use it, be sure to explain it clearly to the nonspecialists first. Make them feel like they belong in the conversation.

ACRONYMS: DROWNING IN ALPHABET SOUP

I only survived my first three months at NASA thanks to a site called acronymfinder.com. Like any large bureaucracy, NASA cranks out new acronyms—words formed by the initial letters of other words—on a daily basis. If you work for a scientific or technical organization or a law firm, chances are you're confronted by an endless stream of acronyms used to make life easier for specialists so they can speak and write in shorthand. Think of acronyms as another form of jargon—they can make work more efficient for some, but create confusion for others. Acronyms often exclude nonspecialists from the discussion.

As NASA is both a technical and a scientific organization, the acronym learning curve is rather steep. I had to learn NASA-specific acronyms like SOC (Security Operations Center), SCaN (Space Communication & Navigation), LCROSS (Lunar CRater Observation Sensing Satellite), and EDLR (Entry, Descent and Landing Repository), and also had to figure out information technology industry terms like IMS (Incident Management System), CTAP (Cyber Threat Analysis Program), PaaS (Platform as a Service), FDCC (Federal Desktop Core Configuration), and CAG (Consensus Audit Guideline), to name just a few. Consequently, someone working in climatology at the Agency might not understand an information technology term unless it is properly explained. The climatologist is a specialist—but he's not an IT specialist.

Acronyms become even more confusing when the same set of letters is used to mean different things in another application. I think of an Automatic Teller Machine when I hear "ATM," whereas the Chilean CTO I mentioned in Part II assumes the speaker is talking about Asynchronous Transfer Mode.

Acronyms make specialized material more difficult for nonspecialists to comprehend because as they read or listen they are dedicating energy to understanding the acronym rather than focusing on the content. The official rule most style guides will tell you is to spell out the acronym on first use. You could write "OS (operating system)" then thereafter write only "OS." I don't especially like this rule. I've written many documents with dozens of acronyms . . . and if the audience is not familiar with them, their workload has been greatly increased. You can't expect nonspecialists to learn ten or twenty vocabulary words up front and then expect them to be able to recall them as they are integrated into your content. Use your judgment when deciding when to use acronyms or when to spell it out. If your document looks like alphabet soup, chances are you need to hold back on the shorthand.

SHORTER SENTENCES, SHORTER PARAGRAPHS, SHORTER CHAPTERS

To enhance the readability of your document, you'd be best served by writing shorter sentences in shorter paragraphs in shorter chapters. Longer sentences and paragraphs may make you appear more educated and sophisticated, but like big words, they create unnecessary roadblocks for readers. Our Internet culture encourages this kind of brevity.

With that said—this brings us to one of those murky areas that mark the difference between rules and guidelines. If this book were written with only short sentences, you'd be bored. Too many short sentences can make content monotonous. Variation is key. Mix up your text by writing a couple of short sentences followed by a more elaborate one. Think about making your text look less dense, but don't sacrifice the quality of your writing.

It's more essential to follow this guideline with more technical documents. Consider an instruction manual or a white paper discussing a scientific discovery—you want those as simple as possible for your audience to access. The longer the sentences, paragraphs, and chapters, the more likely you are to lose them. I've taken some liberty in this book with those issues. I would think differently if I were writing for a corporate client. My belief is that you, my audience, are more likely to be in a relaxed frame of mind—like most people are when reading a book—than if you were perusing a technical document. But note—my sentences, paragraphs, and chapters are much shorter than they would have been if I wrote this book a decade or two ago.

DEVELOP CONTENT THAT SYNCS WITH YOUR AUDIENCE'S CULTURE

Your communication style may require adjustments if you're reaching out to a global audience. When I was working in Chile I struggled with writing business letters at first. Since my Spanish wasn't perfectly fluent, my marketing coordinator, a native Chilean, edited everything I wrote. Her biggest complaint wasn't about my less-than-stellar Spanish, but about my brash style of writing. In New York, I sent out correspondence in a pleasant but direct manner. No chit-chat.

In the United States, executives like to get to the point quickly. In Chile, however, my directness was viewed as rude, not efficient. I can still hear my coordinator saying to me: "Frankie, you must throw them flowers when you write!" I was told to offer the executives receiving my faxes words of respect, if not praise, to blend more effectively into the local culture. I quickly learned to add more pleasantries into my correspondence in an effort to be viewed as something other than a rude American.

But you don't need to travel several thousand miles to experience cultural differences. They can occur from one region of the country to the next. They can also be a factor when speaking to people whose worldview is vastly different from yours. You would, for example, probably strike a different style and tone if you were addressing members of the Tea Party one day and the far left faction of the Democratic Party the next day.

As our world becomes more connected, cultural differences are likely to dwindle. Entrepreneur Vinay Rai tells me it's only a matter of time before India, where content tends to be more formal, will fully embrace the increasingly informal digital communication style of the United States. The youth in India are taking on the mobile culture *"like how,"* he tells me via email. "It's all short content, readable only on smartphones. The older generations, like us" (thanks for the reminder of my age, Vinay), "still prefer long text. India is being divided in half but the next generation is winning hands down."

It looks like the days of "throwing flowers" are coming to a close.

MAKE IT ERROR FREE

This is basic communication 101. Errors turn people off. Even if you are a neuroscience genius, you can't expect your audience to appreciate your thoughts if they're presented with error-filled content. Errors can destroy your credibility, no matter how smart you are. Use your spell and grammar check programs, but look out for other problems your personal computer may not catch. Work with a colleague to help you clean up your act.

Multimedia Style Guidelines

The guidelines I provide in this chapter reflect many of the changes occurring in the way we use language in these digitally driven times. Concise, shorter, and more impactful . . . you get the point. Whether you are writing an old school white paper or producing a more contemporary e-document or web page for your audience, the guidelines don't vary much. People want to get to the information they need faster. Print or digital, we all want efficiency.

The nature of digital media, however, encourages content developers to be so brief it can seem like they are communicating in code. That's not good. Think of what Twitter and other social media platforms have done to our language in a span of a few years. Social media shorthand can be lethal if you're communicating to anyone who's just not hip to nuanced jargon. That's bad because this group often includes senior executives and investors who make decisions that make or break projects. Ironically, this brevity, which is very much in line with the millennial concept of communication, is also very offputting to some and can further complicate already complex topics.

Be careful not to incorporate too much of a Twitter frame of mind in your next proposal or report. Great if you can use social media to lure the curious in, but beware that many of today's decision makers still like fully developed thoughts and complete sentences. They might be shorter sentences, but they are complete sentences.

VI

Humanize Your Communications

Who would you rather watch on YouTube: Steve Jobs or Bill Gates? *Bloomberg Businessweek* columnist Carmine Gallo bets you'll pick Steve Jobs. The late co-founder of Apple Inc. had a magical touch when introducing his innovations. If you attended any of his legendary product launches, you wouldn't hear engineer babble about technical details. Jobs used simple and concrete words. He was clear and concise, and when appropriate became emotionally charged. His presentation style was the polar opposite of his rival Bill Gates, who was more technical. Gallo notes: "where Gates is obtuse, Jobs is clear. Where Gates is abstract, Jobs is tangible."[1]

Jobs did more than follow the basic guidelines of simplicity and clarity like those outlined in the last section. He incorporated those virtues into his own personal style—appearing to live the digital age mantra. Bill Gates is still very much a genius. I applaud him for his contributions for driving technological change, but he doesn't explain or inspire in the same way as his rival. Jobs's natural communication style made him a poster boy for digital age communication.

We don't write copy or give presentations like we used to. Gone are the days of dense, heavy text that weighs audiences down. Likewise, the era of dry, formal presentations that put colleagues and clients to sleep is also, mercifully, coming to an end. Digital natives don't have the time or interest in reading copy that feels like it's rooted in the Victorian era, nor will they listen to a speaker drone. The Internet has jolted us into a contemporary frame of mind where content is more relaxed, easier on its audience, and gets to the point quickly. But be careful . . . relaxed doesn't mean unprofessional. Nor is today's breezier approach appropriate for all situations. Finding a digital age communication style that fits you and best serves your audience may take some effort to develop.

This part of the book is about helping you find your digital age voice. Consider this a communications makeover. The Internet is changing how we share data and express ourselves. The technology that makes heaps of information immediately available is also transforming the way we use language. If you grew up during the yesteryears of analog communication, you may consider adapting your style to more dynamic times. If you're a digital native you may have a relaxed vibe built in, but continue to read. Today's looser style has its limits.

The move to dynamic, friendly content can be unsettling. Those of you born before Gates dropped out of Harvard or Jobs quit Reed College were taught that sounding intelligent meant communicating in a stilted style. Our teachers encouraged us to adopt a seemingly pompous tone when writing. The more elaborate the words and the longer the sentences the better—this is how we marked intelligence. This is most unfortunate. Sounding stuffy doesn't make you smarter, it only makes you harder to understand. To communicate content with ease, leave all that fuss behind. For the new millennium, unshackle the bonds of dense language and discover a freer mode of expression. And be yourself.

16

Find Your Human Voice

Back in the 1980s the corporate clone style was the rage among professionals. We wore three-piece pinstripe suits and sought to distinguish ourselves by blending into a larger corporate culture. Individualism was frowned upon. Like our fashion, our communications styles were equally stiff. When we wrote documents and spoke before groups, we strove to project an image of the corporation we were representing. Our language was often stuffy and impersonal. Writing in first person was practically forbidden. Too bad if our communications efforts failed to explain issues with clarity or inspire our audiences to take action. It seemed more important to emanate seriousness.

Those days are gone. Professionalism has been redefined. The Internet culture has freed us from a rigid, impersonal way of doing business. As entrepreneurship boomed in the last decade of the last century, it became okay to take a more casual, personal tone when discussing matters of importance. You can now humanize yourself, your company, and your brand without suffering rejection from monolithic institutions. You can even get bank loans and find investors while expressing your personal style.

BE A HUMAN

It just so happens that the radical notion of making content more human is what learning specialists recommend. The serious, stilted, impersonal style of yesteryear is not conducive to helping content developers deliver meaning. People work harder to understand subjects when they feel engaged in a conversation. If they feel alone, left unengaged as they receive information, they are less likely to be motivated. But create a situation where they feel as if they are interacting with a visible author, and boom—they engage at a deeper cognitive level.[2]

Crafting your own unique voice that shows your humanity yet retains a professional tone is essential to win over audiences. Don't be a faceless entity devoid of emotion or character. Develop a personality with distinct viewpoints so your audience can engage with you on a personal level. Let them know that you're human—communicate with a tone, style, and pitch reflective of your own distinctive voice. Striking the right style will put your audiences at ease and help you develop a relationship with them.

Adopting a more human style may be more difficult than you'd expect. Seasoned professionals who learned how to write decades ago may find that it's not so easy to put the formal, impersonal stuff in a box and move onto a style more befitting the digital era. Making the transition will require lots of practice, so be patient. I'm not talking about a few cosmetic changes to your writing—I'm suggesting taking on a new persona. Flipping the switch from impersonal communication to speaking human requires developing a personality that some might not be comfortable with. We've been hiding behind a corporate veil so long that finding the perfect voice that represents whom we want our audience to engage with can be uncomfortable.

Tips for Communicating Like a Human

To get the process started I recommend experimentation and practice. Write a lot and speak a lot, but pay close attention to listening to your voice.

▷ BE GENUINE. Open up and let the real you emerge. Share experiences that make you sound like a real person trying to get through life just like everyone else. Think of ways to make yourself authentic. Tell people stories where you come across as an Average Joe who faces learning opportunities and struggles. Never brag or put yourself on a pedestal. Audiences are adept at spotting fakes, so be truthful, not pretentious.

▷ EXPERIMENT. Engage in a playful experiment of communicating with different voices. Push yourself to see how you can let your human self emerge.

▷ LISTEN TO YOURSELF. Practice your new voice and listen to how it sounds. Read your content out loud. Is it written by someone you find engaging?

▷ DIG DEEP FOR CLARITY. Your new voice should resonate with clarity. Remove all the unnecessary fuss and reduce your content to simple thoughts.

WRITING IN FIRST PERSON

Speaking human often means writing in first person—as if you, your actual self, is engaging in a conversation with your audience. People respond to documents written or presentations given from the perspective of "I" or "we" (first person plural). This casual style of communication resonates with audiences because it's less stilted and more real. It fits nicely into the "be human" approach because it avoids the awkwardness that can accompany the formality of third person (he, she, or it).

This book is written in a combination of first, second, and third person. I want to be your human guide—to walk you through the journey of becoming a supercommunicator. First person helps me be more real. Yet if I wrote in first person only, this book would quickly grow tedious. Alternating between first, second, and third person creates energy to keep the book lively.

In your professional pursuits you may still encounter people and organizations that reject the use of first person in formal documents. In some cases you could challenge the system and shake things up with a more human tone. In other situations, emoting too much humanity and informality could spell trouble. Like many of the suggestions in this book, use your judgment.

A Lesson in Humanity from Dame Judi Dench

In the 2012 comedy/drama The Best Exotic Marigold Hotel, *we meet Evelyn Greenslade, a British woman of retirement age who finds herself with financial problems following her husband's death. In a touching scene, we see Evelyn, played by Judi Dench, speaking on the phone to a customer service representative. As she tries to explain her situation, Evelyn tells the representative that she is recently widowed. The person on the other end of the phone shows no compassion. The representative presses on, sticking to the company's script, offering no acknowledgment of Evelyn's loss, let alone empathy.*

Out of financial necessity Evelyn moves to Jaipur, India, and checks into the Best Exotic Marigold Hotel. Ironically, she lands a job at a call center coaching customer service representatives. We see Evelyn conducting a training program where she tells the group how hurt she was by her unfortunate call a few months earlier. She explains to them how important it is to show humanity when speaking to customers.

It continues to amaze me how disingenuous the customer service representatives are at one of this country's largest cable/Internet service providers. When I speak with them, it's like they're trying to not be human. When people call a company, they want to talk to real people—not to highly scripted robots devoid of personality or compassion. The call center employees were pleased with Evelyn's remarks. We learned that they are good people, just focused on their tasks. They never thought about taking the time to be human. Whether you're working as a customer service representative or developing content, remember that humans like to be treated like humans.

17

Speaking Human . . . Without the Human

The reason people struggle with physics is that the subject confounds a lot of our everyday expectations. Chad Orzel, physics professor at Union College, says the challenge of his job is "to find ways to translate physical ideas from mathematical equations into concepts drawing on everyday language and experience." His response to this challenge was to create a distinctive voice: a dialogue between himself and Emmy, his German Shepherd mix.

Talking to a dog about physics? Just think about it: Quantum physics and relativity work in ways different from the everyday world around us. You have to get people to look at the world from a different angle so they're not bringing too many preconceptions to the discussion. Dogs don't have preconceptions. "If you can learn to think like a dog, to approach the world as an endless source of surprise and wonder, modern physics is much less intimidating."

Orzel's books do everything that's prescribed in this chapter—he breaks down barriers between himself and his audience by sharing his relationship with his dog. He and Emmy speak with simplicity in a tone that's genuine. Anyone who loves dogs—myself included—is immediately engaged in the story . . . even though it's about a topic they would most likely find disinteresting.

EMPLOY A SPECIAL AGENT TO TELL YOUR STORY

Not all situations lend themselves to you personally being front and center. When engaging an audience from a corporate position, for example, you can't have everyone speaking in first person. It would be downright chaotic for Shawn from accounts receivable, Alyssa from marketing, and Trevor from IT to open up to you on a human level when they are representing a company of 10,000. But there is a way to reap the benefits of communicating in a more natural dialogue, without getting too personal.

Marketers put human faces on companies all the time by developing personas that serve the same purpose. In the United States, think of Flo, the lively salesperson who hawks Progressive Insurance seemingly anytime you turn on the television. The subject of auto insurance, not an especially exciting topic, becomes more palatable for consumers thanks to Flo's personal warmth and freakish enthusiasm about her product. She becomes the face for Progressive. Consumers are drawn in to the commercials because they like Flo; she's a familiar person to them.

You can adapt this strategy to your explaining opportunity. Consider the mascot employed by Google's Android operating system (see

Figure 17.1). Google knows that people, especially Millennials, no longer read instructions. Yet they have to explain to consumers how to use their smartphones. A dull tutorial isn't going to work. People get their new phones and want to start using them immediately despite the fact they may not know how it works. Android's mascot takes the role of educator here and walks users through a quick tutorial explaining the various features of the phone. It may sound silly, but people respond to this approach.

Figure 17.1 *The Android operating system mascot serves as a pedagogical agent to help users better understand how to work their smartphones.*

Adult educators call persons or icons that guide you through a complicated situation *pedagogical agents*. Using them makes perfect sense to anyone trying to optimize learning. Humans are always searching for ways to make sense of new content, and employing one of these coaches is a great way to make a meaningful connection.[3]

18

It's Story Time!

Terry Goodwin needed to help thousands of employees get over their resistance to new information systems. The year was 1997 and his company's veteran employees weren't comfortable adjusting to new ways of doing business. The Internet drastically changed supply chain management, and the executives at Ryder Logistics needed to take action. "21st century logisticians will evolve into fully competent operations managers and information technocrats," the organization mandated in a statement.[4]

Plenty of employees, however, weren't ready to give up "doing it the old way." Operations managers had to learn new systems. Failure to "evolve" would have been devastating for the company. As Ryder Logistics' senior manager of training and education, Goodwin needed a clever way to make sure the naysayers understood the importance of their company's digital conversion.

Then the idea came to Goodwin. After re-reading Eliyahu Goldratt's *The Goal*, he thought that maybe an instruction tool in the form of a learning novel would be their best way to inform employees. A piece of fiction, *The Goal* tells the story about a manager tasked with turning around his plant's operations in three months. Readers, often college business students, follow a cast of eight characters as they implement change. Goodwin liked the book so much he decided to use the concept of a fictional novel as a means to educate Ryder Logistics' employees on the benefits of information technology in their industry.

Ryder Logistics hired a writer and published *The Janz Awakening*. Following *The Goal*'s formula, *The Janz Awakening* tells the story of how characters Bob and Ralph come to understand their company's new requirement to put computers on every truck. The two central characters are convinced the whole plan is a foolish whim dreamt up by MBAs to raise expenses and destroy their profitability. As the novel progresses, Bob and Ralph come to see the light—information technology will save them money and effort. Goodwin, now retired from Ryder Logistics, tells me *The Janz Awakening* was a successful learning tool because "it was written in first person present tense and put the reader inside the head of the main character."

What happens when a speaker kicks off a presentation with a good story? People put down their assorted "i" devices and listen. It's story time! Ryder Logistics personnel did just that. They embraced the story and learned about the benefits of change as a result. Possibly the most natural teaching device ever created, storytelling is a great way to educate as you entertain. Stories make ideas real—they give our brain something to latch on to that helps us put foreign concepts into a context we can relate to. But when you hear a good story none of that seems to matter—we don't know why we're engaged—we just know we are.

Stories have been told since before Romans wore togas, but the coming of the digital age has rekindled our interest in connecting with this time-honored tradition. With so much data being hurled at us, our brains need relief. Stories give us that break and help us make sense out of what otherwise might just be noise. Perhaps you've noticed that I like to tell stories as I explain complicated subjects to you.

You may be surprised to learn how many organizations use storytelling as a means to communicate complicated content. From buttondown executives to the most brilliant of scientists, communicators are discovering that stories help them get their point across. Many see the narrative as an antidote to these complicated times. American poet Muriel Rukeyser tells us, "The universe is made of stories, not of atoms."[5]

Attention Serious Professionals: You Too Can Benefit from Storytelling

David Rejeski directs the Science and Technology Innovation Program at the Woodrow Wilson International Center for Scholars. His job is to explain topics like nanotechnology, synthetic biology, and bioindustrial ecology to several audiences, including the U.S. Congress. He acts as a liaison between academia and the worlds of commerce and government, explaining topics that befuddle most nonspecialists. "Storytelling and narratives are absolutely critical to science," he says. "The public uses stories to understand science, and so do scientists."[6] Rejeski stands out among professionals working in cuttingedge science and technology. The world would be a much easier place to understand if specialists comprehended the power of storytelling.

The rise of the narrative isn't New Age "feel good" rhetoric. There's scientific evidence that suggests storytelling is very helpful to learning new material. "Stories," write adult learning experts Carolyn Clark and

Marsha Rossiter, "are powerful precisely because they engage learners at a deeply human level." Because they draw us into an experience, we see content at more than a cognitive level. You can depend on good narratives to "engage our spirit, our imagination, our heart."[7]

Additionally, stories may evoke other experiences we've had at earlier points in our lives—and that's a good thing for learning. To learn, we must connect new content to experiences we've had in the past.[8] Telling stories makes those experiences real again. Similar to analogies, stories help your brain latch onto something old so the new content isn't so foreign.

STORYTELLING CAN LIGHTEN UP THE DRIEST OF SUBJECTS

Perhaps you don't think economics is an exciting subject. Many people find it boring; yet two economists figured out a way to use storytelling to keep readers engaged. Daniel Yergin and Joseph Stanislaw tell the story about how politico-economic events shaped the twentieth century in their book *The Commanding Heights: The Battle for the World Economy*.[9] Readers worldwide devoured the historical account like a steamy E. L. James novel.

The Commanding Heights employs a cast of no less than thirty characters—real-life economists, heads of state, central bankers, and finance ministers—as the book's protagonists. The authors explain the pitfalls of big government and the enduring fortitude of financial markets. Yet when you read the book, you become absorbed in the stories told by Yergin and Stanislaw. They introduce interesting people and, like a good novel, you want to find out what happens to them. *Fortune* says the book "reads like a juicy nonfiction soap opera."[10] But while you read the narratives, something incredible occurs simultaneously: you're learning about a subject of academic heft.

The Commanding Heights demonstrates how narratives can illuminate an otherwise bland subject and make it interesting—and therefore accessible. But stories are also a great way to motivate people. Paul Smith, author of *Lead with a Story,* says companies like Procter & Gamble, Wal-Mart, and Hewlett-Packard are embracing the power of the narrative to take action. "You just can't tell people to get motivated," he observes, "you have to lead them there." By telling employees stories you make a human connection that may encourage them to act like the person you're talking about. Their empathy may spill over. "The best way to get the attention of a business audience," says Smith, "is to quickly introduce a main character they can relate to, and put the character in a challenging situation or predicament."[11]

Storytelling in a Digital Age

Multimedia Is Great for Storytelling

Storytelling started out as an oral tradition. The printing press then breathed new life into the narrative, giving us short stories and novels to enjoy and thus expanding audiences. Now multimedia offers storytellers a wonderful new milieu to explore. Multimedia can enrich storytelling. Your audience can savor and appreciate stories in a new, digitally driven way.

If you're delivering content online, embedding it in an e-document, or presenting it live, new digital tools can provide your audience with a more robust experience. Give them more sensory input. Encourage them to see, hear, and even touch your story dynamically.

Offer Your Audience an Audio Experience

Stories feel more real when you hear them rather than read about them. Click here and find out how the accident survivor describes her ordeal in her own words. Listen to the emotion in her voice. Hear the wail of sirens in the background. Or regale your audience with a less serious tale told with a funny accent or more expressive tone. It's like bringing back the golden days of radio.

Use Photos or Other Still Images

People like to see images. Enhance your storytelling by showing actual photographs of the people or places involved. Maybe include a map that traces the sequence of events. Give them concrete images to latch on to that enable audiences to develop a solid picture of what you're describing.

Incorporate Video

The YouTube phenomenon can't be ignored. People are intrinsically drawn to video. Produce your own little drama with actors to tell your story. Generate action that engages. Let them see the sights of the location you describe or visualize your subject that's beyond words. Or give them real-time video that tells the story itself.

Animate

Like watching a Saturday morning cartoon, people relax when they see animation. It takes us back to our youth—a much simpler point in time. Animation can be used to explain some very serious subjects, however. It is ideally suited for more abstract topics where video and photographs may not work.

But . . . Not So Fast. Don't Let Multimedia Distract!

Maybe the scariest story you ever heard was when you were sitting next to the campfire listening to one person and not in front of a monitor experiencing Hollywood's best special effects. Yes, multimedia can be a great way to reach your audience . . . but it can also sidetrack audiences, overwhelm them, and even backfire. The old-fashioned way to tell a story—with no audio, visual, or interactive enhancement—can sometimes be the best approach.

Incorporating multimedia into your storytelling can be a great leap forward. But with any new medium or technology, people often abuse it. A single orator telling a story with the right voices and gestures can easily beat out the most sophisticated multimedia effort. Knowing when and how to incorporate multimedia successfully depends on your audience, the subject, and the situation.

GETTING STARTED WITH STORYTELLING

The benefits of storytelling are many, but it may take practice to seamlessly weave this technique into your communication efforts. You may start out clumsy at first if you've never used stories in a professional setting, but with practice it will feel more natural in no time.

What kind of story should you tell? One that is relevant to the audience and pertinent to the subject being discussed. Don't tell stories unrelated to their topic as a means to break the ice. Some speakers like to kick off presentations with jokes about the traffic, the weather, or a funny thing that happened to them on the way to the conference. They may get a chuckle from the audience—perhaps easing the relationship between speaker and audience. But content that doesn't help you deliver meaning is essentially wasted time. You can do much better.

Tell a story that's in context with the rest of your presentation or paper. Help your audience comprehend your topic at a human level before digging down into detail. The intro story should get the audience's attention and possibly strike an emotional chord, but those feelings must be related to the subject at hand. Your opening story is a great chance for you to communicate at a human level. Don't waste the opportunity.

Look for stories that relate to your subject and include a human element. Use the model of so many of the stories in this book, if you like.

> *A professional encounters a communications challenge.*
> *To overcome obstacles, he explores possible solutions, and then*
> *triumphs by figuring out the right formula.*

Could it be any easier? In each chapter, the characters, situations, and solutions change. Yet like a romantic comedy, the plot remains essentially the same.

Communicators have been applying the "Conflict-Crisis-Resolution Model" for centuries. This tool can help you frame your story easily. This model, also called the Freitag triangle, identifies five stages of a story[12]:

1. THE EXPOSITION. Begin your story—set the stage by providing background information that is important to the story's development.

2. RISING ACTION. Build your story with a conflict or event your audience will find compelling.

3. CLIMAX. Let the conflict reach a crescendo. This is where your rising action comes to a head.

4. FALLING ACTION. Ease your audience down after the big climax.

5. RESOLUTION. Tie up any loose ends.

You can simplify the model to include just context setting (exposition), rising action, and conclusion if that sounds easier.

Tips for Storytellers

As you refine your storytelling skills, consider these tips:

▷ Never apologize for telling a story. Smith says this sends a message to the audience that your story isn't valuable. Apologizing suggests you're wasting their time by telling it. Be confident.

▷ Don't say, "I'm going to tell you a story." Be smooth; naturally work your way into the narrative and just do it.

▷ Use concrete details. Make the story as real as possible. Humanize it by giving the names of real people and places. Include details about your characters that make them come to life.

▷ Increase the number of stories you tell, but don't go overboard. Smith says most of us tell stories "about 1 percent of the time." He recommends that about 10 or 15 percent of your time giving a presentation or 10 or 15 percent of your content should be dedicated to storytelling.

▷ Use your judgment. Not everyone takes this art form seriously. You can still find critics who think storytelling is amateurish or unprofessional. In some rigid circumstances, not everyone may be inclined to hear a narrative. Know your audience.

CHAPTER

19

Testimonials:
A Supercommunicator's Win-Win

I n 2002 the American public knew little about animal cloning and we needed real people—mentally stable, articulate, and intelligent individuals—to speak out on our behalf. I was working with my long-time colleague Suzanne Turner of Turner Strategies to help client Genetic Savings & Clone introduce the world's first cloned house pet. With our effort, CC, short for CopyCat, a brown tabby and white domestic short hair, would soon grace the cover of *Newsweek* and be featured on ABC's news program *20/20*. We anticipated the American public wouldn't be entirely comfortable with the idea of pet cloning. They had all sorts of misconceptions about the science behind it.

"There's a mistrust of scientists and the scientific process," noted our client Ben Carlson, GS&C's in-house marketing and communications guy. "It's difficult for popular culture to keep up with the science. That's why we see popular culture—movies and books—grappling with these issues and helping people process their fears by depicting these horrific scenarios." Scientists in movies are usually depicted as the people creating the problems, not solving them. That means trouble for scientists when they try to explain something new. Looking back on CC's birth, Carlson reflects, "People were inclined to fear what we were doing and mistrusted us."

It became clear that in order for the public to overcome misconceptions we had to talk to them about the science of animal cloning. We couldn't go too deep into the mechanics of cloning, but had to give enough information for them to realize "it's reproduction, not reincarnation."[13]

The semi-scientific explanation was important to our media outreach, but just providing information about the process wasn't enough. Equally important was telling the stories of real Americans who wanted to clone pets. The pet owners, mostly dog people, told us they have or had a pet they thought was their perfect companion. The pet was ideally suited to them—often a dog of unknown parentage with qualities the owner treasured. You can't go to a breeder and get a dog that's "a breed of one." Through cloning, GS&C would become the breeder of that distinctive breed. Pet enthusiasts were willing to pay a lot of money for a mutt that exhibited qualities similar to an original pet.

As we got close to CC's birth, we produced a series of short videos of pet owners who had already donated their dog or cat's DNA to GS&C. We gave them a platform to discuss, unscripted, their reasons for wanting their pet cloned. They delivered heartwarming testimony about how much they loved Rover or Fifi. They all described their pets as unique and told how they wanted not an exact replica of the animal, but a pet with similar characteristics.

The pet DNA donors were uniformly sane and articulate. They had sound reasons for wanting their dogs and cats cloned—and expressed them. The videos reflected their level-headedness, together with their passion for their pets. When CC was born, we offered their testimonials to newspapers, magazines, radio, and television. We tried to hook up local media with donors located in their region to make the story closer to home. The personal stories resonated with the media; not only did we get local coverage, but big-time global exposure on outlets like CNN.

Testimonials—from a communicator's perspective—serve as character references. They're statements that testify that the person making claims or explaining the science is credible. They're real people expressing thoughts that support the point you're trying to get across. In the case of GS&C, we couldn't use the pet DNA donors to explain science—they wouldn't have the credibility themselves to pull that off. However, they did us a tremendous service by assuring the public that GS&C wasn't a crazed organization about to unleash an evil plan. The testimonials grabbed people's attention with a warm story about pets and established our clients as good people. That gave us an opening to explain the science behind the experiment.

Testimonials are a personal favorite for good reason. They're like buying two supercommunicator tools for the price of one. You benefit from the storytelling technique as described in the last chapter, plus you benefit by humanizing your story with real experiences from real people. You can't beat that!

Tell stories of how real people came to understand—and ultimately embrace—your idea. In the case of GS&C, our testimonial team acted like a warm-up band at a concert. They got our audience relaxed and put in the right frame of mind to hear our story. Heartwarming narratives or claims of a product's effectiveness are powerful devices. Take a break from explaining the nuts and bolts of your operation and give them people they can identify with to help you build your case.

You, or the content pro you're working with, may benefit by bringing in a nonexpert third party to explain your complicated subject. You could be the definitive subject expert, the most knowledgeable person alive in a given field, but that doesn't guarantee success in explaining the complicated. People find value in hearing from folks just like them. They put themselves at greater ease listening to someone who's walked in their shoes. They could be a bit leery about the fancy technologist, professor, or scientist who seems just a bit removed from their daily lives. Often, our testimonial friends can't deliver our entire message, but they sure can give us a helping hand.

20

Case Examples That Make Learning Real

Not all delegates participating in the working sessions at the World Intellectual Property Organization (WIPO) have as much specialized education or professional experience as some of their peers. Periodically, representatives from some of the world's poorest countries meet up in Geneva with their counterparts from wealthier countries to debate matters of intellectual property rights—patents, copyrights, and trademarks—and hopefully come to a consensus on how those matters should be handled on a global level. But some delegates from countries lacking the strong legal infrastructure of places like Germany, Australia, or Japan arrive with a steep learning curve ahead of them.

There's a lot of misinformation floating around WIPO's head-quarters when the world comes to visit. Like any other United Nations agency, there are also many political agendas being pushed. Mike Ryan, a client and former director of the Creative and Innovative Economy Center at the George Washington University School of Law, and I hosted a series of informational luncheons to help explain how intellectual property can help developing economies grow. Our programming was desperately needed. We had our adversaries, a few nonprofit organizations working hard to convince developing country representatives that intellectual property rights are the tool of the industrialized world meant to keep poor countries poor.

Ryan and I believe if a country wants to develop a modern idea-based economy, they must develop the infrastructure to protect creators and innovators. Patents, copyrights, and trademarks are necessary tools to prevent the creative class from being ripped off. It's difficult for a runaway pirate economy to gain an economical foothold if boot-leg goods dominate the market. But explaining the benefits of intel-lectual property to some WIPO delegates is a communication challenge. Our adversaries do a great job convincing them we're noth-ing but evil capitalists.

In WIPO working sessions, the delegates are buried deep in the details of intellectual property law. Our plan was to break them out of the minutiae for an hour and a half and offer them a higher-level view of the subject. Our strategy necessitated making the benefits of intel-lectual property come to life. We wanted to humanize this otherwise boring discussion about law and economics. To help us explain the crippling effects of piracy and theft, we invited creators and innovators from emerging growth countries to tell their stories. If the delegates could meet people who've been stifled creatively because of intellectual property crime, went our theory, they may come to appreciate our point of view. It was important that we featured talent from develop-ing nations so the delegates could better relate to their experiences.

For one event, we invited Bobby Bedi, a filmmaker from Mumbai, to talk about how bootleg DVDs of his films have impacted him negatively. Bedi's *Bandit Queen* won critical acclaim at the 1994 Cannes Film Festival, yet despite the accolades, he says making movies in India's Bollywood is still a struggle. Illegal copying of DVDs in India is a big problem. Pirates sell 90 percent of all videos bought in India.[14] A 2009 report produced by Ernst & Young India for the United States-India Business Council (USIBC) estimated that movie piracy and theft are so bad on the subcontinent that 80,000 jobs are lost.[15] Producers like Bedi produce relatively inexpensive escapist entertainment or subsidized art-house work[16] because their films aren't financially successful. How can a filmmaker turn a profit in this environment? Who would want to invest in such a project?

Bedi and other Indian film producers are pressing Indian central and local governments to commit to fundamental reform of anti-piracy efforts by calling for establishment of an independent enforcement body. Anti-piracy efforts in India have tended to be localized and sporadic, say Indian film producers and distributors.

We thought Bedi's story would resonate with our audience. Burgeoning film industries are trying to emerge around the world, but they're often sidelined because intellectual property theft prevents them from making profits. Nigeria's film community "Nollywood," for example, is vibrant, but is stuck because their piracy rate rivals India's. Bedi struck an emotional chord with the audience and warmed the stage for Mike Ryan to deliver his bigger picture discussion about intellectual property rights.

By presenting a case about a real person sharing his real struggles, we were able to reach our audience. We could see the delegates listening carefully to Bedi's story. Later, we discussed with them what they learned and its impact on their lives and role as influencers of the world's intellectual property system. We were pleased to learn that we opened the door, maybe just a crack, but enough to turn on a few lights.

I call this variation of storytelling a case example. You may be familiar with business cases or case studies used by business schools or companies. Case studies are a favorite among educators because they simulate the real world. They sharpen analytical skills, but also condition learners to *think like* people in the example.[17]

The case studies you're likely to work with at the graduate school level are often well-developed pedagogical learning tools. Harvard case studies, for example, are filled with extensive, well-researched content and can take years to produce. My version of case examples is far less detailed and more relaxed. I borrow from the case study format a few key principles that fit my specific needs.

Tips for Using Case Studies

▷ **CASE EXAMPLES ADDRESS PROBLEMS.** Case studies used in academia and in books focus on real problems. That's what makes them powerful learning tools. Choose a "true to life" problem that resonates with your audience. Make it real and make it honest. Make the problem the focus of your communication effort. All content should ultimately contribute to trying to solve the problem.[18]

▷ **CASE EXAMPLES THRIVE ON DRAMA.** Take advantage of the storytelling technique. Engage your audience in a narrative that will capture their attention with real or fictional characters.

▷ **CASE EXAMPLES ENCOURAGE PRACTICAL THINKING.** Present your audience with facts and encourage them to apply those principles to new learning situations.[19] A good case transcends the example you're providing and elevates learning.

Case examples share similarities with testimonials, but unlike testimonials, there isn't any kind of commercial relationship. The people who spoke about wanting their pets cloned on behalf of GS&C were customers. They wanted cloning to advance to a point where they could have their pets cloned. All honest people—none were paid for their endorsement—they became great spokespeople for us because of their genuine interest in our cause. Case examples, however, are stories with no commercial interest. We're not looking for anyone's *testimony* to enhance our credibility or sell a product.

21

What Not to Do When Speaking Human

A DC-based writer friend, James Barrat, author of *Our Final Invention: Artificial Intelligence and the End of the Human Era*, tells me writing is the next thing to be mechanized. Robots, he says, will be smart enough to do some of our writing work by around 2020. A company called Automated Insights is already using artificial intelligence platforms to sift through large database sets observing patterns, trends, and insights. It then turns findings into plain English—prose so good it mimics human communication in tone and personality.

Following up on Barrat's lead, I called Robbie Allen, Automated Insights's CEO. He admits that he has the technology to take data and turn it into content that reads like a human wrote it. His service will be especially important to people doing financial or sports analysis—people who can benefit by a summary of data written in prose. This will make it easier for them to understand big data at a more human scale. The beauty of Automated Insights's product is that "nine out of ten times," says Allen, people can't tell whether what they're reading was written by a person or by artificial intelligence.

The "speak human" style isn't a fad, nor is it an idea that will go away anytime soon. As life gets more complicated, the marketplace seems to find new ways to humanize the intimidating world of big data and bring it down to human scale. As our world gets more technical and increasingly complicated, our inner-cavemen will seek out content that feels natural and unprocessed.

How much of yourself should you reveal when trying to "speak human"? How "real" do you need to be? There's a fine line between emitting humanlike qualities that audiences adore and coming across as narcissist no one wants to associate with. Don't fall into the trap of droning on about your life and your personal quirks. And . . . most certainly never brag. Ego-driven behavior distracts from learning and alienates people.[20] Your readers are more likely to respond to you if you show them your human self . . . show them an experience that helped you learn or grow as a person. Don't go on about your perfect academic record or list of awards received. The trick is to give the right amount of social clues that humanize you but don't become the focus of your effort. This is harder than you may expect. Logically, you might think it would be easier to "be yourself" when communicating. But it's not. Becoming the voice of your content requires finding the right balance between human and professional—and it's no easy task.

Many best-selling business books become bestsellers because their author has figured out how to explain their subjects while guiding you through a journey in a friendly, personable way. The author wants you to feel connected to him. In his book *To Sell Is Human*, Daniel Pink offers up a few bits and pieces of his life to his readers. We learn that his nine-year-old-son, for example, hates showering after baseball practice. Pink doesn't brag about his work as Al Gore's speechwriter or about his time at Harvard; he gives us "slice of life" nuggets of what is real. His readers connect with him because he shares experiences we can all relate to . . . like a stinky boy.

Pick up a few popular business books and see how much the author chooses to reveal. Pay deliberate attention to what they choose to say about themselves and what they omit. Notice how long they spend discussing items of a personal nature or an experience. You'll see that they give you a quick glimpse into their world—enough to make them real—but never too much to invade their privacy or distract from the point of their book.

NOT FOR EVERY AUDIENCE ON EVERY OCCASION

We've learned that you'll be far more approachable and engaging if you lighten up. However, there are still plenty of occasions where a free-spirited, humanistic approach doesn't work.

Many academics and technically minded folks still think humanization, especially when authors use words like "I" or "we" in professional or scientific circumstances, is still taboo. It's easy to find formal, densely written text in these elite circles. Many professors and high-level researchers eschew a casual tone, insisting on text that reads more scholarly. But the tide may be shifting. Penn State University Professor Joe Schall did an informal survey of forty journals pulled from his university's technical library to see if the authors of serious academic articles dared tread into the less formal territory of first person. He checked a range of less-than-blockbuster journals such as *European Journal of Mineralogy, Spray Technology and Marketing,* and *Water Resources Journal* and came up with some surprising results. He discovered that in thirty-two out of the forty journals he surveyed, the authors "made liberal use of 'I' and 'we.'"[21] Schall concludes that this principle of third-person-only is either outdated or is in flux.

I still exercise caution with technical reports intended for official or legal purposes. There were several situations at NASA—like a research paper I ghost wrote—where a relaxed, first-person tone would have been lethal to the project's future. Too much of a human element could have been perceived as amateurish. Attitudes toward formality are changing, even in academia. But caution still needs to be exercised. The breezy approach I suggest to explain content more clearly isn't always the optimal choice with the button-down folks. Let me be clear: Audience awareness is crucial to determining just how human you can become with your style. Understand who's on the receiving end of your communication effort when deciding how humanized you want to be.

Format can also influence the formality of your document. White papers, somewhat authoritative reports used to understand problems or solve issues, are usually long, formal, linear, data-centric documents where you feel experts talking down to you. White papers were the standard communication tool for thought leaders like management consulting firms to help clients understand complicated issues while showing off their intellectual prowess. But busy executives no longer are interested in reading thirty-page papers. Digitally driven media, like e-books, e-articles, and other multimedia creations, are freer, easier, visually appealing communications broken down into small chunks for easy skimming.[22] Overwrought executives are more inclined to peruse documents in this format in our new digital age. Generally speaking, they find the e-book a friendly read versus the white paper's formality.

VII

Getting an Audience to Care

How much more meaningful would my meeting with the Chilean CTO have been if he talked to me about how the Internet was going to change my life? His discussion about how Asynchronous Transfer Mode works was meaningless to me because he didn't make the discussion about the technology relevant to anything in my life. Had he explained that *la supercarretera de información* would change the way I research, communicate with colleagues, shop, and view content, I would have perked up.

Executives love to talk about their companies. Many can go on for hours describing their product lines, qualifications, and financial objectives. But here's the thing: No one really cares about a company or an issue except the people who are connected to it. Customers don't sympathize with logistical or operational challenges; they only care about what affects them. Most investors don't want to get into the nitty-gritty of a business—they just want returns. This is not selfish—this is the way humans think. Unfortunately, executive hubris sometimes gets in the way. People who should know better are more interested in showing off rather than communicating.

To explain anything to an audience, you first have to earn their attention. Hook them with an emotional plea, a good story, or a promise of a better future. Make sure you begin your presentation or document with issues that are relevant to them. We humans are naturally programmed to seek out meaning before we're able to pick up on finer details. Introducing a key idea up front is essential before piling on additional points.[1] If there isn't practical usefulness for what's being explained . . . bye-bye, it's time to check out. We listen to things that can affect our jobs, our health or our home life. To get an audience to care, find something that interests them, then link it back to the subject of discussion.

22

The Power of Personalization

How much money does your doctor take from pharmaceutical companies? Fortunately, my general practitioner's practice only received $750 in 2010 and another $750 in 2011. But there are many other medical professionals who make a hefty sum pushing pills from drug companies. A Nashville psychiatrist, for example, earned over a million dollars since 2009 chatting up products from four different pharmaceuticals to thousands of medical professionals at lectures.[2] It's a nice addition to his financial portfolio, but not an entirely ethical action, as he never divulged his financial relationships with the four companies.

I learned how much money my doctor's practice received by using a "news application" called "Dollars for Docs" built by ProPublica, a newsroom that prides itself on producing important stories with "moral force."[3] The web-based outlet's success is largely owed to its news applications, which offer the public an interactive experience with data. I visited http://projects.propublica.org/docdollars/ and entered the name of my doctor and my state. Within seconds I was able to learn what money my doctor received. I was relieved when I saw it was only $750—a sum not worth getting upset about. But if I found that he earned tens of thousands of dollars . . . I may have had to question his ethics. I don't want the person who's charged with looking after my health possibly prescribing medication based on gifts from drug companies.

Scott Klein, ProPublica's editor for news applications, says tools like Dollars for Docs are becoming increasingly popular because they help personalize the news. News apps help you "attach what you know to what you don't know," he says. By looking up your doctor you become connected to the larger story. "We think a lot about behavior design," Klein adds, "about how we get users to understand the journalistic story we're trying to tell with data while also giving them the chance to explore the data themselves." By giving users the opportunity to discover a personal connection to the story, ProPublica helps make the bigger issue more tangible. The user is now a part of the story.

The Washington Post's Dana Priest agrees. The award-winning investigative journalist says news applications help "bring [the story] into a personal space that's important because it makes the story more real for people." In her critically approved report "Top Secret America," she featured applications that let users investigate their proximity to intelligence gathering organizations. We'll learn more about Priest and "Top Secret America" in Chapter 31.

WHAT THIS MEANS TO YOU

Bringing meaning to audiences is the essence of effective communication. When producing any communication piece—whether it's on paper or digital—it's your job to make sure the content is relevant to the people who are on the receiving end.

I was taught an easy way to bring meaning to prospective clients at one of my first jobs. As a language center director with Berlitz International, I was trained on how to present information while "painting a picture" for prospective students on what their lives would be like with newly acquired language skills. If the people sitting before me could only imagine the benefits of the gift of a new language, goes the theory, it would be easier to convince them their investment would be well spent. We were taught how to sell using "fact" and "benefit" statements. First you tell them a fact (our language programs are fast) and follow it up with a benefit (that means you will speak Spanish before you leave on your trip).

Think the phrase *what this means to you* the next time you're developing content or getting in front of a group. You don't have to utter or write those same exact words, just use that phrase to develop a benefits-oriented mindset. Get the audience to try to imagine how they would profit from whatever it is you're trying to sell them. Is there a way you can discreetly insert benefits into your statements? Can you figure out a way to make the features resonate by helping them see what your topic means to them? Consider these feature/benefit statements as examples:

> ▷ Amazon Web Service gives you access to Amazon's massive infrastructure. *What this means to you* is you can use their resources to get otherwise costly services on demand instead of building applications yourself. This will save your company money.

▷ NetJets offers charter flights for CEOs like you, who wish to avoid paparazzi or protestors. *What this means to you* is that your identity and destination will always remain confidential.

▷ The Toyota Prius gets 49 miles per gallon. *What this means to you* is that you'll not only spend less on gas, but you'll be doing less damage to the environment.

"But I'm not a salesperson," you may be saying to yourself. You may not be selling a product per se, but you are selling an investment in someone's time and attention. So yes, you are a salesperson if you are creating content that needs to engage or influence. To hook your audience, think in terms of features and benefits. Ask yourself why they should care about the information you are to impart. If you can't think of a reason to include a piece of information, maybe you shouldn't include it.

Simple? Yes . . . but effective. Communicators need to spell out benefits for people on the receiving end. Hit them over the head with statements that help them understand what all the facts and figures mean to them. Don't leave it up to your audience to figure out your subject themselves. As smart as your audience may be, chances are they aren't doing the simple addition of putting together the ideas connected to your issue as thoroughly as you have. People pay attention when they comprehend there's something in it for them. Do your job and help them get to the "aha" point of realization.

23

Rational Thinking Isn't Always the Rational Choice

"To get the outcome we wanted, we had to get consumers fired up and pissed off about something that was bad for them. We had to lead them down a path so they could then understand why they should be pissed off." John Cangany, director of Digital Strategy at APCO Online, is passionate about his job, especially when it comes to getting information into the hands of people who need it.

Getting consumers fired up is what Cangany does best, as evidenced by his efforts to prevent a merger that would have created the largest wireless carrier in the United States. Cangany used social media to reach out and touch consumers and convince them that AT&T's proposed $39 billion acquisition of T-Mobile USA would be bad for them.[4] "AT&T was counting on uninformed customers to remain complacent when they announced plans to merge with T-Mobile," he says. Funded by AT&T competitor Sprint, Cangany's mission was to thwart the merger by convincing consumers that the acquisition would reduce competitiveness in the wireless industry. Cangany says the merger would make them pay more. "The crux of my job was to take this complex issue and distill it down into something that made sense to a whole bunch of different kinds of audiences, then get them to care enough to do something about it."

AT&T is a formidable opponent. It maintained that T-Mobile was a fading competitive presence and that the merger would increase competition by offering an "interim solution to the spectrum shortage"[5] that was resulting from the explosive growth of wireless data services. But others didn't see it that way. Sprint and other wireless carriers believed the transaction would have delivered a deathblow to the competition and higher prices to consumers. The merger, they feared, would give AT&T too much market power and diminish their own ability to compete effectively with AT&T in the wireless space.

Regardless of which side of the argument you want to believe, this merger became a transaction where emotions were riding high. In his efforts, Cangany developed a social media campaign to help inform cell phone users what the proposed business deal would mean to them from a Sprint point of view. He used social media to not only educate people about the topic but also unite them. Get the information out there in easy-to-understand language and visuals and motivate consumers to take action. Their website, www.notakeover.org, offered several easy ways to speak up to Congress and the Federal Communications Commission (FCC) to let them know the American people did not want this merger to go through.

In his campaign, Cangany made sure he was upfront about all of his claims. He said he posted nothing that was inaccurate or biased. Everything he did, he assures me, was transparent. Ultimately, he believes, consumers gravitated toward his message because they believed No Takeover was telling the truth. "It came out that AT&T

was funding groups to speak in favor of the merger through grants made by AT&T Foundation. Once it was perceived that AT&T's testimonials were biased, we gained the upper hand," noted Cangany. An AT&T backlash ensued and consumers became concerned. People, says Cangany, "believed the arguments about the need for competition and demanded a marketplace with more choices." Cangany's group earned the upper hand in this high stakes game of emotional wrangling.

The more powerful the emotion, the longer someone is likely to remember it. Research in neuroscience and the field of "intrinsic motivation" proves rather definitively how critical feelings are when it comes to memory.[6] It's up to you—the communicator—to evoke and sustain interest. If you can do this, your audience will follow willingly.

There's no better example of emotion being used as a tool to coerce than in U.S. politics. Unfortunately, for the television-viewing public here and in other democracies, political strategists have used emotion as a weapon to conjure up strong feelings to get you to vote for their candidates. Politicians saturate our programming with unrelenting ads prodding us to become enraged on topics ranging from gun rights to immigration laws to taxes so we'll support them. Emotional pleas can easily run amuck.

In his book *The Political Brain*, Emory University Professor Drew Westen observes that we usually don't vote for a candidate who doesn't resonate with us emotionally. "From the standpoint of research in neuroscience," he writes, "the more purely 'rational' an appeal, the less it is likely to activate the emotion circuits that regulate voting behavior."[7] Citing psychology powerhouses like Darwin, Skinner, and Freud, Westen claims that humans are inclined to be led by emotion. "The brain is not a dispassionate calculating machine objectively searching for the right facts, figures, and policies to make a reasoned decision." In essence, our rational selves are willing to push aside facts and act on emotion. The political strategists are correct in appealing to a voter's passions rather than his intellect. We may not like how politicians play with our emotions, but they have the proof that it impacts the way we vote.

If you want your audience to engage in your presentation, website, or other effort, an emotional plea may be just what's needed to wake them up. Hopefully, however, you can pull this off with more decorum than our politicians. Research confirms that not only will you get their attention from the start, but you're likely to create a memorable experience for them that can lead to more permanent learning. Although this method has been proven extremely effective in getting people to care, don't rush too quickly to toss emotion around like it's a cheap commodity. Toying with peoples' emotions is tricky business, and if you don't do it properly it can backfire. The consequences can be ugly if you don't show respect for your audience and they feel you're putting them into a vulnerable situation.

Credibility is essential when playing the emotion card. If your audience knows you, is familiar with your organization, or learns to trust you, your chances for pulling off an emotional plea are greatly improved. Transparency is also critical. If you want your audience to believe you, make certain you have no skeletons in the closet. Everything you put into the public domain must be truthful and backed up with credible references. The Internet is making us savvier in our ability to spot fakes. As we become more efficient readers thanks to the Web, we're also becoming more skeptical about claims made by others. Digital natives are especially tuned in to matters of credibility and transparency. Always be forthright.

Some organizations are naturally suited to employ emotional pleas in their communication efforts. Think of anyone trying to get you to take action on a hot topic. Groups interested in encouraging us to be more mindful of the environment come to mind. Their fear plea is a good one: "If we don't act more respectfully of Planet Earth, we're going to destroy it." Organizations focused on animal survival, human rights, and crime can easily incorporate emotion into their outreach campaigns with minimal effort. But getting people to care about topics that are less volatile becomes more of an art form.

KNOWING WHEN TO EVOKE EMOTION

Deciding when and how to use emotion is subjective. More writers and speakers can benefit from injecting evocative content into their outreach efforts. But, like many of the tools discussed in this book, an emotional plea can backfire if you misuse its power.

Consider topics like the environment, human rights, animal protection, politics, and religion fair game when trying to stir up feelings. We see how the media tugs on our heart strings to get us to care about malnourished children, public television's survival, and rising sea levels to get us to open our check books. Other topics where there isn't as organic of an opportunity—like accounting or teaching a technical function—don't lend themselves to emotion as easily. Most communicators could do a better job putting some sizzle into their efforts, but other times it would look stupid to attempt to conjure up feelings for an inanimate object or a boring subject. Imagine how silly you'd feel trying to evoke emotion when explaining to someone how a toilet works. Be reasonable.

There are also times when audiences won't want an emotional plea from you. I learned this lesson the hard way when writing a strategic plan on cybersecurity. The client intended the document to be a tool to convince management that big changes were needed to protect the organization from cyber theft. They had already experienced hackings and lost valuable plans to foreign companies and governments. They needed to do more to thwart future attacks.

I read up on the cybersecurity crisis that many companies and governments are currently fighting. I also dug up information about attacks on the organization I was hired to help. After a couple of days of research I was in an emotional state. Cybersecurity is scary stuff. Hackers can destroy nations and corporations from a laptop. With so much input in such short time on the subject, I felt compelled to speak up on the severity of this problem. I wrote an emotionally compelling two-page introduction to the seventy-five-page plan.

I explained the explosion of malicious code threats, gave hard numbers on the costs of security breaches, and even cited examples of attacks at their own organization I had read in *Businessweek*. I described how the world's largest corporations and governments are at risk of losing the cybersecurity arms race in a concerned, but not hysterical, voice. I calmly stated the facts and explained that taking action is an imperative that must not be delayed. The tone of the paper was professional, but clearly written to make readers understand the significance of the topic.

My client's boss, however, didn't see it quite that way. All of the emotion-provoking content in the introduction was stripped out before the final version was distributed. I was politely told that "there is no room for emotion in this kind of document." I disagree with this action. I believe the people who would decide the budget for cybersecurity spending should understand the severity of the issue—and if it takes making an emotional ploy, so be it.

Many organizations believe that using emotion to get people to care is not professional. This is not true. I'm sure there are many times when communicators err in their judgment and play the emotion card unnecessarily or foolishly. But there are many opportunities when writers and speakers could be so much more effective by getting their audiences to care with an emotional tug. As a looser style of communication continues to evolve, we'll see a greater use of emotion in the workplace. Loosening up may not come easily to the most straightlaced of organizations, but gradually we'll see more people use this tactic.

Building Blocks
and Analogies

S ometimes the content we need to explain requires a bit more
effort than what I've described so far in this book. Simplicity and
clarity are great first steps. Making the content relevant to the audience is also helpful. But if you're trying to teach a technical process or
need to get into the nitty-gritty of a complicated subject, you may
need to pull a few more supercommunicator tricks out of your bag.
This part focuses on two tools I find essential to helping people "see"
complicated subjects without the benefit of graphic visualization.
Sometimes our best tools to explain the complicated are our brains
and our words.

Building blocks, or *layering*, helps us dole out bite-size bits of information in moderation. We take one simple idea and gradually put it
on top of another idea, giving our audience the chance to absorb new
material. We increasingly add slightly more complicated ideas as we
progress. Comfortably, we break through barriers of bafflement and

disbelief by taking one step at a time, until they reach a higher plane of understanding. We never force our audience to digest too much information at once. Like climbing a mountain—look at the short path before you, not the entire route to the peak.

Analogies are another tool that can bring comfort to a bewildered audience. If you can't explain what something is to someone, then maybe you should explain what something is like. I used three in the last paragraph—did you notice? You're probably familiar with analogies from high school literature class. Building on the art of comparison used by poets and novelists for centuries, analogies in business, science, and technology can bring instant awareness to an otherwise floundering audience.

In the digital age, these timeless literary devices still matter. While new visualization tools help us to see complicated subjects from a new perspective, graphics can't do it all. Effective communicators benefit from lessons from the past and use layering and analogies to help them deliver meaning.

CHAPTER

24

Building a Path to Comprehension

Electricity, unlike water or gas, cannot be easily or inexpensively stored; it's typically generated as needed. Precision balance is required to ensure a consistent and ample flow of electricity to meet consumer demands. Systems operators work around the clock to coordinate resources among thousands of electricity providers. A successful systems operator not only needs to have a practical understanding of the physics of electricity and mechanics of the electric system but also needs to be schooled in the complexities of regulatory framework. Good instincts that experience brings and the ability to make appropriate decisions quickly are also essential to get the job done.

In previous generations, line crew employees were typically considered the best candidates for managing the electric grid. Today that is no longer the typical progression. "A workforce change has brought with it a communications and training challenge: men and women who don't have utility experience or sufficient knowledge about electricity from a practical perspective are approaching systems operator positions from a much different starting point," observes Pamela Ey, adult learning specialist at SOS Intl, a leading provider of training and compliance services to the energy industry.

"We now have a lot of four-year engineering-degreed folks coming through our training programs," adds Rocky Sease, CEO of SOS Intl. "Their professors gave them the necessary foundation but there are very few places in the United States where you can get an understanding of how the grid works and how all the pieces fit together. They know the individual pieces . . . but when you start talking to them about how to relate to power flows across the grid, that's a whole different way of assembling the information that isn't necessarily taught in college."

It can take five years for a systems operator to really get to know a system. SOS is able to speed the process. Their training programs start with the basics: studying how direct current and alternating current work. This initial training serves as a building block for the next step: understanding the process of how electricity is moved from one location to another. As students begin to grasp the basics of electricity, SOS trainees transition their newly found knowledge to the next level: examining what the laws of physics permit in terms of energy flow.

Complexity is heightened when regulatory issues are added to the equation. The operator must understand balancing authorities' boundaries, which may sometimes require unique procedures performed under certain conditions. The learning process continues as SOS's clients layer the pieces. They grow to understand how those issues need to work seamlessly so consumers can flip on the light without thinking about where their power comes from.

Without layering, SOS trainees might feel overwhelmed, needlessly struggling with abstract notions. The goal of SOS's programs prevents that by distilling the elements of physics down to their roots. Sease and Ey introduce regulatory and other issues at an equally basic level. From there they build from the foundation, reaching for a higher understanding of how electricity gets generated and delivered. Whether they call it layering or apply the concepts without labeling it, most institutional trainers embrace this approach. Layering breaks big, unwieldy concepts into bite-size morsels that prevent audiences from gagging on too much information. Building new ideas on top of what is already known eases the sting of comprehending the complicated.

LAYERING LETS YOU BREAK DOWN THE COMPLEXITY OF A SUBJECT

When a subject is truly complicated we need to nurture our audiences to help them comprehend. Raise them to a more mature level of understanding, but do it gradually. Help them along by using the building block technique. Eager to jump to the big idea, writers and presenters often get too complicated too quickly, leaving their audiences mute with confusion. In a presentation, you'd expect the bewildered to speak up and say: "Hey, you lost me in the first minute!" But this doesn't happen—people don't like to look uninformed among peers, clients, employers—or anyone else. It seems safer for them to just keep silent. Adult learning specialists Ruth Colvin Clark and Richard Mayer advise you to "help the learner manage the complexity by breaking down the lesson into manageable segments—parts that convey just one or two steps in the process or procedure." They recommend we "minimize extraneous cognitive loads so that learners can allocate limited working memory resources to learning."[1]

If your audience doesn't have the prerequisite knowledge to understand your idea, you have no choice but to give them a tutorial to help them build a path to comprehension. Invest a few paragraphs at the beginning of your paper or a few minutes at the start of your presentation to lay the groundwork. By breaking down your complicated story into manageable chunks, you can construct building blocks. Think of a complicated idea as the sum of smaller, easier-to-comprehend nuggets of information. Reveal the building blocks to your audience at a gradual pace—let them acclimate bit by bit—not revealing the entire 50-story building or 12,000-foot mountain all at once.

Each step is a block of knowledge that's useful to understanding the greater topic. Let your reader or audience member take one simple step at a time. Let them take a subject they are already familiar with and add on an increasingly difficult layer of complexity. Keep building layer on top of layer, step by step, taking what is already known and expand on that knowledge. Build a staircase to your ultimate complexity.

The goal is to make the abstract attainable not in one swoop but through a graduated, more digestible, approach. When we encounter a new concept our brains intrinsically scour our memories looking for a similar experience to attach the new situation. That is, the brain "looks for" connections to earlier information so it knows where to store new sensory input. Adult learning specialists Kathleen Taylor and Annalee Lamoreaux write in an article "Teaching with the Brain in Mind" that our brains want to find existing patterns that appear to "make sense" of an idea and thus be more likely to be remembered. When a brain can't find a commonality, it can't forge meaningful links to existing patterns.[2]

Tips for Layering Your Communications

In layering, you search for a series of simple steps that can lead your audience to an understanding of something they have never encountered. This exercise forces you to not only comprehend the essence of your subject, but to understand the entire framework the concept is built on. A superficial understanding isn't going to work here. That's actually good. You'll be a better communicator if you comprehend the details lying beneath the surface.

▷ EMPATHIZE WITH YOUR AUDIENCE. Consider how much background they'll need to grasp your topic. Think carefully about what background is essential.

▷ RETRACE YOUR STEPS. How did you learn this material? If you can reconstruct the layering approach you followed to gain mastery of the subject, maybe the same will work with your audience.

▷ BREAK DOWN YOUR SUBJECT INTO BITE-SIZE PIECES. Distill the big idea into smaller, more manageable pieces. Create a schematic to see for yourself how one piece of information serves as a building block for another piece of information.

▷ CONSIDER COLLEGE TEXTBOOKS AND THE INTERNET AS TOOLS TO HELP YOU SIMPLIFY. Sites like Wikipedia do a great job in getting through the clutter that can bog you down.

▷ NEVER OMIT ELEMENTS OF THE STEPS IN YOUR EXPLANATION. Doing so could compromise accuracy. Layering is about simplification through steps, not about dumbing down.

Look to the Movies for Examples of Layering

Hollywood does an excellent job of bringing moviegoers up to speed using the building block technique. The audience needs to be brought up to speed on background information. Without crucial prerequisite knowledge, the audience could flounder in ignorance and disbelief. Screenwriters and producers are tasked with making the plot seamless and believable.

Consider Arnold Schwarzenegger's 2000 action film The 6th Day as an example of layering in the movies. Set in 2015, fifteen years after the film's premiere, Schwarzenegger plays Adam Gibson, a man who comes home to find a clone living out his life. Gibson stumbles into a conspiracy led by the evil conglomerate Replacement Technologies attempting to take over the world with its clones.

The premise for this movie would have been downright absurd if screenwriters Cormac and Marianne Wibberley had launched into the plot without providing sufficient background. A generous amount of time was devoted to introduce the character and his world early in the plot's development. In setting the stage for the unbelievable, the screenwriters were able to keep audiences seated for the entire film.

The 6th Day begins with an easy-to-grasp scenario. We learn that animal cloning is widespread in 2015. This fact is reasonable because four years before the film was released, Dolly, a domestic sheep, became the first mammal to be cloned. Consequently, moviegoers watching The 6th Day would have found it perfectly reasonable in 2000 to assume that by 2015 animal cloning could have been possible, and even common. The acceptance of the existence of cloned animals becomes the first layer this film uses to build credibility.

The screenwriters take concepts believed reasonable in 2000 and add onto their audience's knowledge base bit by bit. The entry point to our trip of understanding in The 6th Day is that animal cloning is scientifically possible and may be widespread by 2015. In the next layer, Adam's dog Oliver helps bring plausibility to the storyline. When the dog is found dead of natural causes, Adam is urged by his wife to take his remains to "Re-Pet" so he could be cloned and replaced before Adam's daughter finds out her pooch has died. In a third layer we learn the daughter not only loves her dog but also wants her own Sim-Pal, a freakishly lifelike "living doll." The doll looks and acts like a real infant. We're informed that the lifelike doll is considered a toy every girl wants in 2015.

If you can accept that animals can be cloned, then why not

believe that you can take your dead dog to be cloned while doing errands at the mall? If that is possible, then it makes perfect sense that by 2015 you can also go to the same mall and buy a toy baby with humanlike appearance and mannerisms. From that point, it's not too far of a leap to fathom human cloning. Schwarzenegger's ensuing battle with the clones seems perfectly believable because of the layered approach. The movie didn't start with clone wars, it started with attainable concepts that got progressively more complex.

The best examples of layering are often those where the audience has no clue the author is using this technique. They may be subconsciously aware of layering, but probably don't think about how the screenwriters were setting the stage. When done well, layering is a seamless ramp, taking an audience from what is known and comfortable to what is yet to be explored. It's an added bonus when they're blissfully unaware of the calculated steps the author has built to lead them to a higher plane of understanding.

CHAPTER

25

The Power of Comparison

A *STAR TREK* ANALOGY TO THE RESCUE

David Pensak, founder of Raptor Systems—now a part of Symantec—is best known for bringing the first commercial Internet firewall to market. A multifaceted innovator with more than forty patents to his name, Pensak faced an uphill battle explaining what an Internet firewall was at a time when businesses and consumers were still trying just to understand the purpose of the Internet itself.

Pensak's inspiration for describing the firewall came from the epic late-1960s television show *Star Trek*. Pensak came up with a brilliant analogy that cut through the novelty of the firewall and explained the concept in a way that was immediately accessible to his target audience. Pensak was fascinated with *Star Trek*'s notion of "beaming" an individual from one location to another. In the show, beaming was a function of a transporter, a teleportation machine that converted people or things into energy (*dematerialization*) and reconverted them back into matter (*rematerialization*) once the energy had been "beamed" someplace else. "When transporting someone, sometimes the transmission was fast and clean," says Pensak, "but sometimes engineer Scotty had problems beaming people and fiddling with the controls was necessary." And the dematerialization/rematerialization process from *Star Trek* happens to be an excellent analogy for explaining the Internet. As Pensak explains, "This fictional invention sets the stage for the reality that with any communication medium you can have static or dropped packets."

The Transmission Control Protocol (TCP) and the Internet Protocol (IP) are the fundamental communication protocols that make the Internet function. TCP/IP enables your computer to send messages to or get information from a mother computer that also has a copy of TCP/IP. Think of TCP/IP as a two-layer program. The higher layer, the Transmission Control Protocol, manages the assembling of a message or file into small packets that are then transmitted over the Internet. The file is received by a TCP layer at a corresponding computer, which then reassembles the packets into the original message. The Internet Protocol, or lower layer, handles the packet address so that your file gets to the right destination. TCP/IP is amazingly flexible and can allow myriad sizes and types of packets.

Pensak found that comparing the transporter and TCP/IP was an effective means of explaining his product to his audience. When a person is "beamed" through the transporter, he's reduced to bits of energy. Those bits travel and arrive in a jumble, and it's up to the machine on the receiving end to make sense of the mess and reassemble the person. Similarly, when we send information over the Internet, it's broken down into packets that are sent and arrive in no particular order. Each piece has a serial number that the receiving end is able to read, enabling it to display the information as it was meant to be seen, in its proper order.

The analogy goes even further by describing problems in the beaming process, providing a platform from which Pensak is then able to explain the need for a firewall. Imagine if you entered the transporter room and someone arrived who was not who you were expecting; or, worse, suppose that you were in the transporter and instead of arriving at your destination, you were kidnapped. People using computers had not worried about analogous possibilities with their Internet messages because they had not conceived of the possibility before. Pensak's firewall, like the transporter, would protect against data getting scrambled or kidnapped in the same way.

"If we had tried to do this without the visual analogy that *Star Trek* gave us, we would have had to teach computer science to people who didn't know and didn't need to know. Our job was much easier as a result," said Pensak. He knew that this analogy would be a sure winner with his audience, many of whom were bound to be *Trekkies* just like him and almost all of whom would at least have watched some episodes.

ANALOGIES = AHA

There may be no more difficult task in communication than explaining a concept for which your audience has no foundation. The basis of what we do as writers and presenters is to break down complicated topics into simpler concepts. That should always be your first step. But what if your audience simply can't fathom what you're talking about despite your excellent attempts at clarity? If they can't grasp what something *is*, perhaps they'll understand what something is *like*. Analogies, explanations through comparison and association, are tools we can harness to link the unfamiliar to what is known, putting our audience at ease.

Analogies are the figures of speech that lead to the "aha" moments of simple epiphany. That's what we're aiming for with our audience. I use the term *analogy* in this chapter to mean a comparison between two ideas that is based on similar features. Metaphors and similes are both cousins of analogies. They, too, are excellent linguistic figures that can simplify explanations of complicated ideas, but metaphors and similes are more artistic and literary, which means that they are less exact. You probably remember writing similes in high school: phrases that link associated objects or ideas by words such as "like" or "as." Metaphors are even more poetic and rely on associating two unlike things. In contrast, a simple analogy—the comparison of two like features—can be both very exact and very effective.

Analogies have been around since long before Aesop wrote his fables, but don't believe for a minute that this old-school trick is any less useful today. Comparisons and associations help us understand new ideas in a way that transcends description. Communicators incorporate analogies into all channels. It doesn't matter whether they're writing a traditional document like a white paper or producing a cutting-edge video for YouTube. Analogies enhance content, especially complicated content, helping your audience make sense of what might otherwise be perceived as being too abstract.

There will almost certainly be times when you can benefit from creating a mental image for your audience. This chapter explains why analogies can be a communicator's best friend, provides examples of how they've been used effectively in real-life applications, and offers tips on learning how to incorporate them into your communication efforts.

YOUR BRAIN CRAVES ANALOGIES

Analogies work amazingly well in communicating complicated ideas. It's all a matter of how our brains work. Research on adult learning suggests that the brain naturally uses analogies to connect new input to existing patterns. As Taylor and Lamoreaux have shown, the brain responds to new situations by asking how the current experience relates to earlier experiences. Our acute, innate ability to evaluate new experience based on stored memories and knowledge of prior situations is an evolutionary advantage unique to mankind. "The human brain," write Taylor and Lamoreaux, "learns to change its own algorithm to account for variations, contrasts, and more integrative metaphors, leading to more inclusive, creative, and flexible responses to unfolding experience."[3]

When we struggle to understand something new—especially if it is complicated—our brains work extra hard to find familiar context from past experiences in order to process the new input. The power of comparison should not be underestimated when attempting to explain a new concept to your audience. Our brains like analogies; in fact, our brains seek analogies. As communicators we need to feed the brain what it wants: comfort food. Give your audience comparisons that they can relate to and it will help their brains digest content more easily.

PAINT VIVID PICTURES

Analogies, along with metaphors and similes, are like poetry and should be used carefully. They can enhance a description or explanation, but in other contexts they may be seen as superfluous and distracting. Knowing your audience is of paramount importance. You need to understand them, as well as knowing what tone is expected for the paper or presentation, before creating descriptive comparisons.

In a documentary, for example, analogies can effectively unpack complex information and help viewers understand content unfamiliar to them. Science writer Eleanor Grant of the National Geographic Channel often uses analogies in her television programs. Grant strives to make her work thought provoking and engaging; she wants her audience to *feel* the science she is explaining. Analogies help Grant with that goal, but she is always careful not to simply pull out some stale, overused cliché. As a documentarian, Grant does have a fair degree of latitude to dream up as many analogies as she can, and she uses that latitude when appropriate in order to evoke an emotional response that will engage her audience. In her 2007 series *Amazing Planet*, Grant paints vivid pictures for audiences:

> This is the Big Island of Hawaii, home to Kilauea, one of the most active volcanoes on Earth . . . and perhaps the best place to see the planet's labor pains as it gives birth to itself.

> For the poet, this lovely dangerous stuff oozing and spitting out of the volcano might suggest a glowing lifeblood pumped from the red, red heart of a hot vital Earth.

> A more apt comparison might be a bad case of indigestion. This is a planet that belches, vomits, and shutters, heaves and passes gas, really nasty gas.

> Whether from a pulsing heart or a heaving guy, lava is our only concrete glimpse into the Earth's interior . . . into an engine of creation and destruction that dwarfs all of the mighty power of the planet's human inhabitants. What lies beneath?[4]

Grant's use of language is powerful and evocative. The analogies she employs are both emotional and shocking. She's trying to create new images—many of them related to our own bodies—to help us feel the power of the Earth and not just intellectually understand it. The language creates the sense for us that the Earth, like the human body, is a living thing. In this brief clip, we hear comparisons to birthing and labor, indigestion, and human anatomy, all in an attempt to punctuate the telling of a geological event. The vividness of the language, which accompanies equally compelling video of an active volcano, can grab wide swaths of the target audience: families. We can easily see people in their living rooms, watching the National Geographic Channel and both learning and being entertained. The analogies add texture, connectivity, and immediacy to the script. Grant relates eruption to experiences most of the audience will have had or at least witnessed. People watching and listening will not need to create new categories in their brains in order to process this information. That's already been done, and everything is made as simple as the actions in our everyday lives.

KNOW WHAT IS FAMILIAR TO YOUR AUDIENCE

Interested in creating analogies of your own? Good. But remember, analogies come with caveats. Analogies can be double-edged swords: they can help your audience grasp new concepts but they can also undermine your narrative if they open up too many sets of meanings, leading your audience down a spiraling path of misconception. And while good analogies are golden, bad analogies only make the complicated more enigmatic. Once your audience has a mental image in its mind, that image is difficult to erase or change.

Good analogies are usually the result of a creative mind that has embarked on a process of free association. The best advice I can give on the topic is just to let your mind go. Think about commonalities between your audience and yourself and see whether you can find a link that makes a comparison possible.

Think carefully about what imagery will resonate best with your audience. Since analogies are about comparisons between what is familiar and what is yet to be experienced, you want to make sure that everyone can easily understand the basis of your comparison. Analogies obviously don't help if you are comparing something new to something equally perplexing. In thinking of what you and your audience share, ask yourself which of the common experiences that you share with them are so natural that they need no further explanation.

Open your mind and let it wander. Think about experiences everyone in your audience can share. Is your audience a largely homogeneous group? If they share similar cultural experiences, work in the same profession, or all grew up in the same decade, you have more latitude to be creative with your analogy. Or is the audience a diverse group made up of people from different cultures, varied age groups, or professionals representing myriad industries? If so, you may need to make your analogy more general.

Make sure your analogy is a complete fit; if anything from your comparison doesn't match up perfectly with what you're explaining, head back to the drawing board and try again. Test your new analogy on friends and colleagues for confirmation that it works. It may take some time to develop the skill of thinking analogically, but you'll be pleased with the results your efforts at free association can produce.

CHAPTER

26

Analogies in a
Professional Setting

The opening night session at a conference on information technology (IT) architecture turned a standard conference presentation into one big analogy. Held at a resort in Kitzbühel, Austria, in the shadows of the snow-capped Alps, the conference was meant to instruct CIOs from some of the world's most prestigious corporations. So it initially felt odd that two architects—building architects, not IT architects—kicked things off by talking about their experience transforming slums in Caracas, Venezuela into livable, low-income housing. Why would the management consulting firm McKinsey & Company choose to open the conference with an exposition on a housing project in the steamy streets of a Latin American city? It was a mystery at first, but in time, it all made sense.

McKinsey's Jürgen Laartz invited architects Alfredo Brillembourg and Hubert Klumpner, founders and co-principles of Urban-Think Tank,[5] to discuss their design for providing basic infrastructure for some of Caracas's poorest inhabitants. The architects encouraged the development of partially constructed buildings to serve as the foundation for inexpensive housing projects. People then would move in to the building shell and construct a unique personal space to their own specifications. The government provided only the most basic infrastructure, namely the shell, but that was an affordable option and a great alternative to the slums. Not only did this program improve the quality of life and sanitation in areas of Caracas, it afforded new residents the opportunity to take personal responsibility for their living space.

Remember, this discussion took place at the opening session of a conference on computer systems. There was not a single reference to IT architecture during the presentation or in the following discussions. The session simply ended. The conference delegates went to dinner immediately after the session, with no specific instructions to discuss the topic. Laartz knew, however, that the guests would take the opportunity to ponder the meaning of the lecture on architecture and discuss it among themselves. Perhaps the guests realized that the message McKinsey was sending them was clear. The CIOs in attendance were all dealing with "legacy" infrastructure issues at their companies. They were at the conference to discuss with their peers how to meet the demands of today's high-speed, web-centric business environment using the aging but "tried and true" technology that is central to their operations. This highly elaborate analogy—comparing building architecture to information technology architecture but without ever making the comparison explicit—was staged by McKinsey to encourage the CIOs to view legacy planning from a different, more innovative vantage point.

As expected, many at dinner worked through the comparison

between the architecture of Venezuelan slums and the architecture of their own systems. Laartz had hoped to push the executives to a higher intellectual level in order to help them prepare to meet the challenges they face in modernizing their systems, and his elaborate analogy seems to have worked. One conference delegate, an information technology director from a Wall Street bank, made a point of telling me about this experience. The analogy proved effective in opening a discussion on legacy systems and providing a memorable experience that delegates could draw on to regain the conceptual momentum of that conference experience.

On the other hand, formal documents, such as strategic plans and budget requests, do not always lend themselves to scintillating analogy. I typically don't use many analogies when working on assignments that call for formality. Many corporations and government agencies expect certain documents to be cut and dried. Executives looking at a budget request, for example, may not be amused by a flowing narrative that compares cloud computing with big fluffy clouds in the sky. Likewise, I doubt that executives on Wall Street or Fleet Street are particularly interested in analogies as a way to describe financial products. Government administrators, business executives, and other decision makers who are pressed for time often don't want to be sidetracked by comparisons or imagery while perusing certain communications. It is possible that an analogy or two might help them see the project from a better perspective, but they may see your insightful comparison as a superficial indulgence instead.

For the executive audience, simple and straightforward should be the default approach. Busy people often like information delivered without much embellishment. It is still true, however, that analogies can be used with everyone, including senior executives. A subtle, light-handed approach can be amazingly effective when a straitlaced approach is expected. Communicating with elite audiences by way of analogies can be tricky, but it is not impossible and, many times, a well-placed analogy will be able to hit your point home in the most efficient way.

Analogies, Metaphors, and Similes Online

The best analogies are likely to be the ones you create on your own. If you know your audience, you are best equipped to think up comparisons that will resonate. If, however, you are having a hard time creating something that works, you might find analogies on the Internet that someone else has dreamt up. Type in the key words of your topic along with "analogy" or "metaphor" and see what's already been imagined. Just remember to give credit to the author or source.

The following pond analogy is just one of many comparisons I have found online to describe how the nation's electric grid works. Remember SOS Intl? Layering isn't the only trick up their sleeve. Pamela Ey and Rocky Sease told me they use analogies like this one to help students who are preparing to work on the electric grid to visualize the science behind electricity.

"The challenge of teaching electricity is that you can't touch it," notes Sease. "When you are starting out on the grid it is hard to grasp that power has to be generated at the same instant it is being used . . . within fractions of a second." Electricity is invisible and odorless. Its intangible nature poses a challenge for grid novices, most of whom had been accustomed to working with more tactile products.

To create an image to show students the instantaneous nature of electricity, Sease frequently uses the following analogy: Imagine that you have a pond that needs to consistently maintain its water level. No matter what happens, that pond must be 100 percent filled, twenty-four hours a day, seven days a week. An increase or decrease in the pond level would be unthinkable. The challenge is that people keep taking water out of the pond. Your job, as master of the pond, is to make certain that all the water going out is immediately replaced by water coming in. It may sound like a punishment from Greek mythology, but your fate is to keep that balancing act going in perpetuity.

If that analogy doesn't do it for you, there are many others avail-able online to describe the power grid. Check out the Beer Model, the Rope Loop, the Band Saw, the Rough Sea, and the Crowded Room, just to name a few. The Internet has a wealth of these helpful hints for any topic at hand.

Visual and Interactive

A s the son of a graphic designer, I appreciate the power of visualization. For about forty years, my dad, Frank A. Pietrucha, created annual reports, advertisements, newsletters, and logos for an assortment of organizations. I would like to believe I inherited his good eye for design, but know I lack his talent on the production side. I didn't pick up the ability to design from dad, but I learned an equally important skill from him. A graphic designer is only as good as the content professionals he works with.

I saw a stream of clients come through our house—where dad, a freelancer, held court. I observed them and got to know them. Inevitably, my father's best designs were created for clients who worked collaboratively with him—not the self-important people who dictated to him what they wanted, but the clients who engaged my father in constructive conversation. The savvy clients provided him with as much useful information as possible, offered lots of feedback, and ultimately wound up with the best finished product.

As a communicator, my job usually entails originating strategy and written content for clients. Like the parade of folks who worked with my dad, I now team up with graphics pros to bring my content to life. The lesson I learned growing up still holds true—the better you work with your designers, the more effective your communication efforts will be. Whether you describe yourself as a professional communicator or a professional who communicates—you can benefit by engaging with the people who work on building your websites, dreaming up your visualizations, and making your content come to life.

Not long ago, it was a crazy proposition for non-IT folks to master their own computer design needs, but more communicators are taking an active role in doing their own design and developing their own applications. If that's you—pay attention, because there's a lot more to generating quality graphics and applications than you may realize. If, however, you never plan to originate a design in Adobe Illustrator or never care to create any type of graphic image, you still need to pay attention. Super-communicators are involved in all aspects of the communication process. We're the quarterbacks providing necessary input and driving the process. Our job is to make certain that whatever the creatives do, it brings meaning to the communication effort. You may not be doing the design or programming, but like the puppeteer Gepetto from *Pinnochio*, you're behind the scenes pulling the strings.

The invention of the personal computer opened the floodgates to a universe projected through a new lens. Our digital age world is filled with visuals and interactive tools. Suddenly it's easier for us to show rather than say in meetings. We can inform audiences by inviting them to participate in the learning process—not just sit back as idle observers. We're adding more graphs and photos to our reports and can even design fliers to advertise bake sales and find lost pets. Multimedia, including online tools and emerging learning experiences like hands-on museums and video games, make new content more visual and tactile. It's a good thing these tools have been invented—visuals and interactive learning help our comprehension. With all the complex subjects out there, we digital citizens need to understand that our brains appreciate relief from centuries of text.

"Vision is our most dominant sense," writes John Medina, author of the bestseller *Brain Rules*. The developmental molecular biologist with a passion for the mind's ability to react and process information tells us that incorporating pictures into our communication efforts helps our audiences grasp content more effectively. "Pictures trump reading every time," he claims, suggesting that people are more likely to remember information when offered pictures.[1] For centuries the written and oral word were our primary communications tools. But it's visual learning that's innate to our behavior. Before books and sermons there were pictures—cave drawings, to be specific. Our minds were wired for visual communication long before the written or spoken word.

We've ignored our inner caveman's cravings for pictures long enough. It's time to level the playing field and realize that vision, our dominant sense, has been neglected. Our brain dedicates about a half of its "available energy" to process visual stimuli.[2] Shouldn't we take better advantage of that? Supercommunicators understand the importance of visuals. They know the written word is far from dead, but grasp that communications, especially those that explain complicated subjects, need to be retooled into dynamic visual offerings.

Perhaps you heard the myth that we're either visual learners or auditory learners. That's right . . . I said *myth*. All learners experiencing a new content area benefit from relevant visuals.[3] Incorporating visuals and interactive devices into your efforts appeals to all. Giving your audience variation with media is a great way to hold their interest and speak to different parts of their brain.

More visual communication is a step in the right direction, but twenty-first-century humans want not only to see information but also to experience it. The movement to bring hands-on learning experiences to the forefront is gaining speed. People don't want to sit back idly reading, listening, and watching—they want to participate. Science center exhibits where children can touch foreign objects or games they can play on their smartphones are popular options. Educators are exploring ways for students to use all of their senses in the learning process. They're trying to figure out how to bring them into the action, instead of observing from the sideline.

Interactive learning is still in its relatively early stages. The research that's been done suggests there are opportunities worth pursuing in this area. But communicators should proceed with caution—many of the exciting new devices that promise learning are frauds. Developing a dynamic teaching tool is harder than most expect.

27

More than a Garnish

Someone calls 911 after hearing gunshots. A police officer responds and quickly finds a man in his car in a parking lot. The cop pulls him over, proceeds to the driver's side window, and questions him. As they're talking, the suspect abruptly takes off and the cop engages in a pursuit down winding country lanes in excess of 100 MPH. We know this account is true . . . it was all captured on the police car's dashboard camera.

The police video shows the pursuit like a made-for-TV cop show. The suspect tries to run the officer off the road a couple of times. They swerve, weaving back and forth. The suspect drives down another road and makes a sudden U-turn. The cop does the same. Eventually, the cop gets stuck in the mud. Moments later, he finds the vehicle but discovers the car's driver has fled on foot. The officer shines his flashlight into a dark field. Where did he go? Now out of range of the video camera, he can't be seen. Then the sound of gunfire rings out . . . The officer is still not visible at this time, but the firing of seventeen shots from an assault rifle is audible on the tape. Glass is shattered. You hear nothing but gunfire disturbing the otherwise peaceful country night.

Moments later, the cop comes back into view on the video. He's been shot. He calls for backup. When additional officers arrive they find a dying cop; a bullet got past his bulletproof vest. The police eventually catch their suspect, but he claims he was only acting in self-defense. He said the cop had his gun pointed right at him and he was afraid he was going to be shot, so he fired first.

A few months later, lawyers representing the deceased officer hired a company that produces forensic animations, three-dimensional (3D) visualizations of an expert's scientific opinion. They poured over the video and ballistics obtained by the police searching for clues. Using laser scanning and other technologies, they reconstructed the incident. They determined it was the ninth of seventeen bullets that killed the cop. Their high-tech analysis took data, analyzed trajectory paths, and made a 3D model that definitively proved where the suspect and cop were at the time of the shooting. The suspect wasn't facing the cop as he said. He was kneeling beside a house in the dark, hidden from view. An analysis of the lighting and visual range for the officer clearly indicates there is no way the cop could have seen the shooter.

Now, try to explain all that to a jury.

This story is complicated. I reduced the plot to the most essential facts, omitting details without altering the outcome, but a jury would have heard all the facts. That's a lot of information for a group of people not schooled in criminology. Jason Fries, CEO of 3D-Forensic, says, "Trying to get this kind of story across to a jury verbally would have been impossible."

A computer animation was produced to illustrate exactly what happened. The animators, working together with other experts, reproduced what the officer could see from his vantage point and what the suspect could see from where he crouched. With the use of this new technology, the jury was able to understand the complexities of this case by seeing an accurate reenactment. They came to understand that the officer's death wasn't self-defense, but an execution. The suspect was convicted and now sits on death row.

Using animation software such as 3D Studio Max and Maya, "reconstructionists" put together a visualization of how the shoot-out occurred so judge and jury could make an informed decision by envisioning the facts.[4] 3D-Forensic shows what would be difficult to explain verbally. The data were made visual and then turned into a multimedia product that told a story.

The visuals made the learning process easier—that's straightforward. If you can see data, instead of just hear or read about it, naturally you're going to understand a topic faster and more effectively. Not only did the animation show the data, but it turned it into a narrative. By developing a reenactment, they visually told the story of how the officer was brutally slain. Stories, as we discovered in Chapter 18, make content more understandable and more memorable. Put stories together with good visuals and you're golden. Talk about a win-win situation for the prosecutors. Not only were they able to "show" rather than just "tell" during the trial, they were able to weave the data into a compelling, plausible narrative that was certain to capture the jury's attention.

GOOD MULTIMEDIA IS MORE THAN A GARNISH

"One of the keys to producing good graphics is to have some sort of focus," Alberto Cairo, author of *The Functional Art,* tells me, "Don't treat graphics like a dumpster where you throw a bunch of data. . . . You have to try somehow to categorize the information and create a proper interface or a narrative. Organize your graphics . . . as if they were pieces in the story." Your graphics need just as much structure behind it as does writing. Without a proper backbone, your visuals will waffle without support.

Cairo spoke to me specifically about his work in infographics and visualization, but what he offered holds true for all graphics and similarly with multimedia-driven communication products. Currently teaching information graphics and visualization at the University of Miami's School of Communication, Cairo is a journalist by training. He attributes many of his accomplishments in this growing field to his background. As a journalist, Cairo wants to tell stories with his visuals. His creations just don't hang out there in nothingness. They have a purpose, not to adorn, but to provide a learning opportunity.

The quality and usefulness of graphics and multimedia should be approached with journalistic sensibilities. Unfortunately, new multimedia adopters don't always think out coherent strategies to marry new digital-age tools to their communication efforts. Their attempts to spice up content often results in the inclusion of sparkling features that bring little or no value to the text. Seeing multimedia as a new form of communication—and not just a few supplementary enhancements tacked on to an otherwise conventional piece—is critical to make these new wonder tools more than a "garnish."

Michael Zimbalist, who founded and runs the New York Times Company's research and development operations, says his organization is moving past using graphics and multimedia like an olive or lime. He regards "Snow Fall," the now famous series (see Chapter 3), as one of the first news features "that embedded multimedia in a really organic way." He told me the *New York Times* had been working hard over the better part of a decade to build the talent and expertise necessary to deliver blockbuster multimedia features. It looks like their efforts are paying dividends.

Zimbalist believes the *New York Times* is helping originate a distinctive new communications form that gets us past our feeble first attempts at multimedia. "We had brought over digital technologies but were still tethered to the linear format of the print story. They were like garnishes, off to the side. Click here for a slide show . . . Click here for interactive graphic . . . Click here for a video . . . 'Snow Fall at Tunnel Creek' showed how these new tools could be organically embedded into the linear flow. That's what made it stand out. It felt like a new form."

For a couple of decades, communicators have been trying to get a handle on how to use new digital tools effectively. Many of our efforts haven't been successful. For multimedia to reach its potential as a dynamic means to educate and decomplicate, we must be more strategic in the ways we use it. Ironically, these tools that we're using to help us make content more interesting are often only a disruption for our audiences.

Distracting visuals and features, adult learning expert Ruth Clark notes, often don't serve much of a function to facilitate learning. Clark found that learners actually do better perusing "basic versions" of documents rather than those that are graphic loaded.[5] But that's because so many documents are cluttered with visuals that are more decorative than informative. Images we think add value to a document or instructional piece may not be effective and can actually deter audiences from comprehending the message.

28

Quality and Integrity in Design

"Too many designers think they know what they're doing with information, but do not," says John Grimwade, the director of information graphics at *Condé Nast Traveler* magazine. From the short time I spoke with him, I could tell he wasn't a mean person, nor was his remark meant maliciously. He takes his profession seriously and wants others to do the same. "There are no data police," he tells me. Infographics are like the Wild West: "We need some kind of people to monitor these things and get them headed in the right direction."

We're emerging from a "dark period of information design," says Grimwade. Business people felt liberated when easy-to-use graphics programs were loaded onto personal computers back in the 1980s. They now had the tools and could create all sorts of documents. But to trained designers, those days were like the big hairstyles of the decade—an aesthetic train wreck. "People had the means to embellish a business document, but not the knowledge to do it in a meaningful way."

Perhaps you've seen Grimwade's award-winning work. Leaf through a copy of *Traveler* and you'll see his creations. Grimwade worked with Oceanic Control in Newfoundland to produce an infographic that illustrates the system that controls 900 daily flights over the North Atlantic (see Figure 28.1). Another infographic from *Condé Nast Portfolio* reveals the medal count from the Athens Olympics divided by the GDP of the country. Grimwade shows that athletes from countries with low GDP, like Ethiopia, Georgia, and Belarus, fared far better in garnering medals at the Athens Olympics than their counterparts from wealthier nations (see Figure 28.2). They are easy to understand, tell a story, and are aesthetically pleasing. But most important, they are purposeful, not adornments. "I'm just trying to turn on the lights a bit," he says. "Graphics can help you unravel the complicated."

DON'T CONFUSE VISUALIZATION WITH ART

Most visualization and graphics you see in the media are developed, as you would expect, by graphic designers. These creative individuals are trained to stylize content to make it visually appealing. That's how we've always seen their role. For centuries, *making things pretty* has been their primary focus. Alberto Cairo says this limited view of graphic design can deter good communication. The former director of infographics and multimedia at *Editora Globo*, the magazine division of Brazil's biggest media group, warns that we need to do more to improve the relationship between visualization and art.

In Brazil, Cairo says, journalists and designers alike call graphics "art." He writes of his experiences working with them in São Paulo:

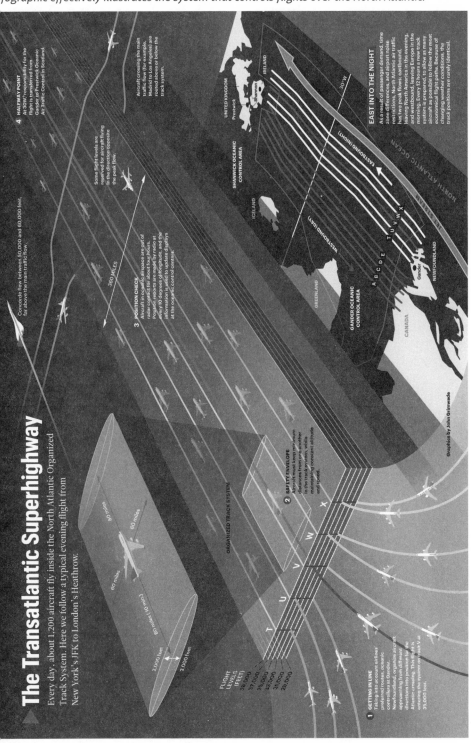

Figure 28.1 *"The Transatlantic Superhighway" by John Grimwade for* Condé Nast Traveler. *This infographic effectively illustrates the system that controls flights over the North Atlantic.*

Figure 28.2 *In "Medal Exchange," Grimwade effectively communicates that deep pockets don't necessarily produce world-class athletes.*

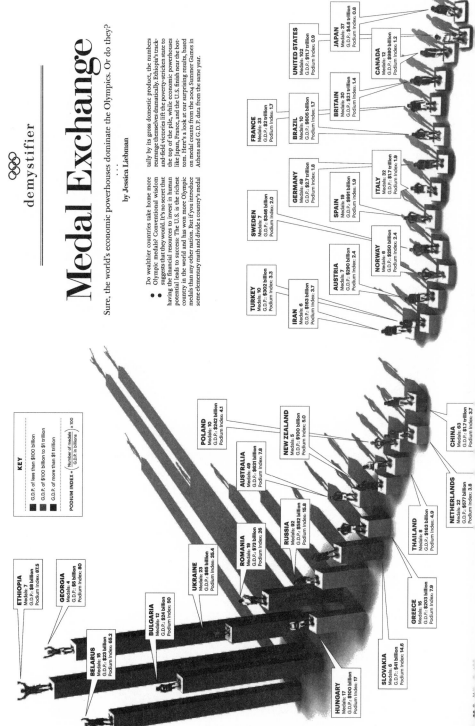

"They would say with that charming musicality of South American Portuguese, '*Vamos fazer uma arte!*'"[6] The translation, "Let's make a piece of art," suggests graphics should be viewed as art, not a serious means to communicate substance.

Jason Fries raised an interesting point in our interview. "We live in a visual world," he says. "Today, people lose interest in verbal. . . . My experience is that to reach the younger people who grew up with everything digital, you have to use pictures." Although I agree with Fries's statement, I must urge budding supercommunicators that they need to be just as focused on creating quality graphic images as they are in delivering excellent written or verbal content. Good graphics can boost your communication skills to new heights; bad visuals, however, will only confuse and obscure your message. And when you are working with information, you have to be really careful.

The challenge with using visuals, however, is that many of us aren't using them effectively. Just because technology gave us the ability to add images to our work doesn't mean communicators are using them wisely. Once again, we come back to the theme of "adding meaning." Caught up in the gee-whiz excitement about digital tools, many of us forgot that good communication means bringing insight to an audience, not glitz. The widespread availability of graphics programs has opened a Pandora's Box of visual stimuli, but much of what's in there has been meaningless adornment.

Guidelines, Tips, and Observations for Multimedia, Graphics, and Visualization Design

No matter what media you're working in, there are a few guidelines to consider when producing visual communications. Make sure your effort packs a punch and delivers meaning to your audience:

Keep Visuals Clean and Simple
· · · · · · · · · · · · · · · · · · · ·

Thoreau's plea for "simplicity, simplicity" holds true when it comes to multimedia design. Keep content uncluttered. Eliminate any visual that does not add to the value of your communication effort. Favor clean aesthetics—your text and images should feel open and breezy, not dark and dense. Your audience will feel welcome to your content if it suggests a friendly tone.

Simplicity is essential. If you can't make a simple visualization that people understand easily, then move on. "I'm always fighting with my graphics people about the complexity of some visualizations," notes The Washington Post's *Dana Priest. "If I don't get it or if I have to work too hard . . . then it doesn't work." But Priest goes on to offer me an example of an exception to the "rule" of simplicity and clean aesthetics. She refers to a map of counterterrorism organizations produced by the* Post. *The first attempt shows how crazily all the organizations were connected and the contorted routes the information flowed between them. The design team originally rejected this first attempt and came back to Priest with a cleaner, easier to navigate map. But Priest rejected the second visualization in favor of the first. "By its nature it's a confusing map," says Priest, "but that's the whole point." She believed the "crazy" map did a better job in telling her story about the intricate relationships among counterterrorism organizations.*

Be Extra Careful When Working with Graphics
· ·

Many statistical graphics we see in the media, even from so-called reliable sources, distort data. This is unfortunate because it leads readers, users, and listeners astray. Whether it's a result of ignorance or malice, it's becoming more of a problem as designers untrained in statistics and other do-it-yourselfers have the resources to communicate data visually. Edward Tufte writes that complex ideas should be "communicated with clarity, precision and efficiency."[7] It can be tempting to orig-

inate a design that influences your audience to observe data favorable to the point you're trying to make. Graphics that show misleading information can be a blow to your organization; you run the risk of destroying credibility. Don't fall into the trap of distorting data.

Avoid Extraneous Images and Items That Distract

Multimedia can make your audience emotionally aroused. That can be a good thing if it boosts their cognitive level of engagement. But stimulation isn't always what the supercommunicator ordered if it interferes with the learning process. Too many pictures—or other bells and whistles—can alter your audience's ability to make sense of your subject. People have limited capacity for input, so don't distract them. Keep them focused.

Matching Zimbalist's "garnishes" reference, adult learning expert Ruth Clark coined the phrase pumpkin graphics *to describe decorative visuals that are thought to add interest or possibly humor to content . . . but fall short on enhancing the overall message.* Pumpkin graphics *is her comical way of describing what results from someone slapping a clip-art jack o' lantern onto a presentation just because the meeting happens to be taking place around Halloween.[8] The smiling pumpkin with missing teeth does absolutely nothing to make the presentation better. It only serves as a reminder of the season and distracts from the purpose of the meeting.*

You Can't "Force" Visualizations

It's easy to get caught up in the excitement of data visualization. This growing field is dynamic and communicators want to be part of the excitement. But a Berlin-based visualization architect I spoke with warns, "Data can have its limits." He tells clients to set realistic goals and understand that results may not be as spectacular as what they're envisioning. "About one in ten data sets can support a visualization piece," he cautions. Not every visualization is going to be epic, nor will they all go viral. He suggests you talk to your visualization pro about what is feasible and understand that you won't know how effective the piece will be until after it's done.

People Like Color

No surprise here. Audiences respond favorably to colorful images. Give them an emotional boost with a splash of color and put them a better learning frame-of-mind. But be careful with your color choices and don't overdo a good thing.

Discuss color with your designer or research color palates on your own. Choose the right color scheme and you can help draw your reader/user into your document. Select the wrong combination and you run the risk of alienating your audience. The wrong color scheme can disrupt their flow and encourage them to look elsewhere—away from your webpage. Amy Balliett of Killer Infographics suggests that to keep graphics cohesive and calming, as opposed to jarring, consider limiting your palette to three primary colors. She also suggests visiting websites that cater to helping people choose the right shades. Her suggestions include Adobe's Kuler and COULOURlovers.[9]

Animate

Animation can be a great way to explain content, especially hard-to-grasp data. In Chapter 17 we learned about the effectiveness of employing an "agent," like the Android mascot, to guide learners through a new process or complicated material. Animation can add a level of "human" connection your audience will welcome. Extraneous animation, that which does not add meaning to your content, however, needs to be stricken.

29

Visuals for Presentations

D r. Anthony Fauci—the director of the National Institute of Allergy and Infectious Diseases (NIAID) who advised us to "know thy audience" earlier in the book—has more thoughts to share about effective communication. As someone who speaks often to large, disparate audiences, he has a good sense about which presentation visuals work and which bomb. He referred me to slides he produced for the Sixth International AIDS Society (IAS) Conference on HIV Pathogenesis Treatment and Prevention in 2011. They offer us a good example of how to use presentation decks effectively.

At the global conference in Rome, Fauci had a half hour to deliver a retrospective of the thirty-year history of HIV/AIDS to an audience of world-class scientists. There were many important milestones to discuss, and several topics he needed to cover in a short span of time.

An immunologist who made substantial contributions to HIV/AIDS research, Fauci wanted to give a talk that would meaningfully summarize the challenges and accomplishments of the period. He wanted to be as informative as possible, but didn't want to lose his audience in the process.

Fauci's first step in producing his slide deck was to develop a timeline matrix. At one end of the timeline was 1981, the year physicians first realized they were dealing with a new syndrome. The timeline continues through three decades to 2011, then extends into the future. Fauci used the matrix as a device to keep bringing the audience back to the story's chronology. Using this simple device, he figured out a way to turn his presentation into a story. It became easier for his audience to comprehend all the information they were getting because of the easy-to-comprehend manner in which it was framed.

Figure 29.1 is an example of Fauci's timeline. In this early slide he acknowledges that the HIV virus was identified as the cause of AIDS in 1983 and 1984. Fauci shows how this important piece of information fits into the chronology of the story just a couple of years after the mysterious syndrome was first discovered.

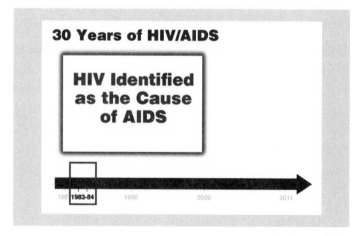

Source: NIH/NIAID

Figure 29.1

As the presentation progresses, the audience moves further down the timeline. A major milestone in the war against AIDS was the FDA's approval of the drug AZT in 1987 (see Figure 29.2). Conference attendees could see where this landmark event took place in relationship to other milestones.

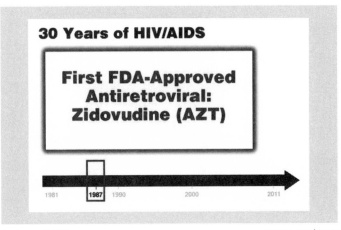

Source: NIH/NIAID

Figure 29.2

The timeline technique worked especially well when Fauci needed to return to earlier dates in his remarks or advance to future dates. He could bounce back and forth through time but still keep his audience centered by always bringing them back to the timeline. This enabled the audience to feel grounded—not unsettled.

But the timeline wasn't the only tool that made Fauci's presentation successful. A photo of a young, brown-haired doctor doing his rounds at NIAID adds a nice human touch to a fact-filled slide deck. He's visiting a patient in the HIV ward surrounded by about a dozen medical professionals (see Figure 29.3). Fauci lightens the somber tone of his remarks by joking that *he* is the doctor leading the rounds— you just can't recognize him because his hair was brown—not the silver it is today. The audience lets out a laugh for this prominent person's self-deprecating comment. The famous immunologist just endeared himself to his audience and made a thirty-year retrospective of a disease more personal.

Source: NIH/NIAID

Figure 29.3

Fauci uses quality graphics to explain some of the more complicated issues in his presentation. Figure 29.4, the slide showing the HIV replication cycle highlighting targets for antiretroviral therapy, may be intimidating to some, but remember, Fauci's audience is made up mostly of medical professionals. I don't understand it, but I'm not an immunologist, virologist, or physician, so that's okay. I am not his intended audience for this presentation. The graphic is clear and easy on the eyes; audience members in the back row can see it without strain. The illustration is not junked up with too much text or other distractions.

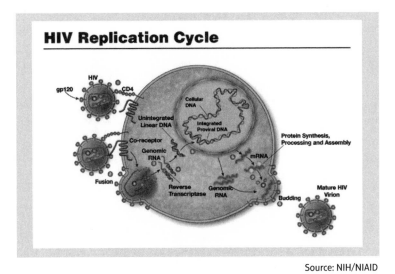

Source: NIH/NIAID

Figure 29.4

The drug AZT helped slow the progress of the disease among patients. But in the 1990s, researchers discover the benefits from a "three-drug therapy" (see Figure 29.5). Fauci explains that the evolution of treatment strategies led to a point where a combination of drugs made the virus undetectable for a sustainable period of time. He projects a graphic that clearly shows how the three-drug therapy is more effective than one or two drugs. Again, the image is simple and uncluttered. The visual makes a point that is easy for the audience to grasp.[10]

Presentation slide decks can be extremely effective communication tools, if they're done properly. Unfortunately, all too often they're not. Presentations get junked up with too much text and extraneous stuff. A lack of interesting visuals contributes to audience malaise and an abundance of bullet points seemingly throws them into a catatonic state. Fauci managed to avoid all of this by producing a thoughtful and engaging presentation. I'm sure it took Fauci and

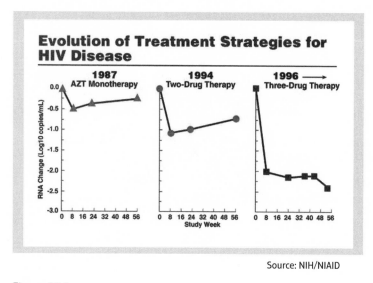

Figure 29.5

his staff many hours to produce these slides. He also had resources that may not be available to all of us. But no one said developing a good presentation is easy.

TO POWERPOINT? OR NOT TO POWERPOINT?

In Chapter 5, I refer to Edward Tufte's tirade against the popular presentation software PowerPoint from his 2006 book *Beautiful Evidence*.[11] If you would like to know more about his beef with the ubiquitous software program, I recommend you read his essay. He raises good points about the danger of bulletizing content and trivializing information. But PowerPoint isn't an evil program. Most of us still use it. "A lot of people think it's hip these days to bash Power-Point," says storyteller Paul Smith. "But that's like faulting the English language for bad political speeches." Perhaps people just need to know to make better use of the Microsoft product.

One of PowerPoint's biggest drawbacks is that presenters use it like a teleprompter for their speeches. PowerPoint gained popularity because it became a tool for people to build their own presentations. It's much easier to deliver a presentation if you put all your key points and data up on the screen and then read from it. They got comfortable using its templates to help them organize their thoughts. In this way, PowerPoint is for many a crutch. It simplifies public speaking for the person at the podium, but unfortunately has become a tedious bore to the folks sitting in the conference room.

In my consulting days at NASA, we used PowerPoint all the time, even after Tufte questioned whether PowerPoint's "cognitive style affect(ed) the quality of engineering analysis" at the Agency.[12] When I worked with the team building Nebula, the Agency's cloud computing platform, we generated a lot of slides using the Microsoft product. Cloud computing was in its infancy—we were one of the first, if not the first, civilian U.S. government agencies to build a proprietary cloud. The newness of this program required our business and technical teams to give a lot of presentations to a lot of people from different backgrounds.

We had a master file of over a hundred slides. If you were to give a presentation, you could pick which slides were relevant to your audience and topic, then dump them into a new presentation. All the slides were formatted similarly so the presentation didn't look like too much of a hodge-podge. Sometimes you'd have to generate a few new slides, but those would be added to the ever-expanding master file for future use. This system worked well for us from a production standpoint.

Producing an effective presentation requires lots of time and effort. It also can require a level of creativity that some can't deliver. The Nebula team was always frantically busy . . . the way we used PowerPoint was efficient from a work management perspective. It just probably wasn't the best tool to inform our audiences.

Tips for Working with PowerPoint

If you decide to continue using PowerPoint please keep in mind a few points:

▷ USE POWERPOINT AS A TOOL TO SHOW IMAGES. Visual learning is important. Make your presentation more memorable by featuring visuals that will elicit emotion from your audience or will somehow bring them greater meaning. Visuals should be compelling and memorable. Images that illustrate a process or help explain an idea are also helpful.

▷ LIMIT NUMBER OF WORDS. Simplify everything. Cut down your text so it reads more like a Twitter post than a white paper. Think headlines, not the body of your subject. Tell your audience what's important . . . don't burden them with reading dense text.

▷ BANISH BULLET POINTS. Bullets are effective in documents, but are lethal when it comes to presentations. Don't truncate your subject to fragmented points. This can alter the meaning of what you're trying to explain.

▷ LIMIT THE NUMBER OF SLIDES. Want to alienate an audience? Subject them to a presentation with too many slides. If you use your presentation software as a tool to show visuals and headlines, this shouldn't be a problem.

ALTERNATIVES TO POWERPOINT

PowerPoint is often our *go-to* when asked to create a presentation, but there are alternatives. Find a tool that you're comfortable with that frees you from a restrictive format. It will require you to be more creative, but will result in a better end product.

When I attended Tufte's full-day communication course I found out from his staff that he presented his visuals in Keynote—Apple's answer to PowerPoint. He only used Keynote as a means to show visualizations and other images. He avoided any use of words on slides. Keynote merely was the tool to help project graphics. I liked the absence of annoying bullets, but my personal style isn't as draconian as Tufte's. I believe use of words, like quotations or simple informational points, can be featured effectively.

Keynote seems to be a favorite among the high-tech crowd, especially the Apple fanatics, as well as designers who appreciate it for its better visual quality and user experience. Designer/blogger Rachel Arandilla gives Keynote high marks for its theme designs, transition effects, graphics, and multimedia friendliness. She, however, cautions users that Keynote can't run on Microsoft, but PowerPoint is available through Microsoft Office for Mac.[13]

I did one of my highly informal, very unscientific surveys among public relations professionals and asked them what they're using for presentation tools. I discovered that while Keynote is popular, a product called Prezi is starting to win the hearts and minds of my colleagues. Now several years old, Prezi displays information in a nonlinear way, offering users greater flexibility. Prezi CEO and cofounder Peter Arvai says his software helps audiences "look at the big picture, then zoom into detail." He likens the Prezi process to how the human brain works . . . suggesting his product is a more natural way for us to learn. The level of freedom it provides is an antidote for the confinements of PowerPoint, but comes with a challenge: Prezi's blank canvas approach can overwhelm less creative types who need more structure. Yes, the danger of Prezi is that it just might force you to think.

Other presentation software is available on the market if you want to check them out. Some of them you are welcome to use free of charge. Consider Google Presentation for simple presentations, Lotus Symphony for basic desktop use, and Impress if you can code in HTML, CSS, and Java Script.

Bring Touch-Screen Technology to Your Next Presentation

Created by the people who innovated touch screens over forty years ago, Elo Touch Solution's 70-inch screens enable presenters to interact with content by touch in real-time. Not a software program like PowerPoint, Keynote, or Prezi, Elo Touch is hardware that allows you to connect with the Internet or one of your existing programs. It resembles the gigantic wall screen systems broadcasters like CNN use on election night or during storm coverage. Stand in front of the monitor to "swipe" and "pinch and zoom" into content you want to highlight for your audience. This tool offers communicators more freedom and flexibility than conventional presentation tools, creating a more interactive environment that is good for learning. A 70-inch Elo Touch screen runs about $10,000.

CHAPTER
30

Let Your Audience Explore

"Complex things happening at all levels we can't see," explains Jennifer Frazier, of San Francisco's Exploratorium. The cell biologist, who lists "plankton" and "visualization" as her latest obsessions,[14] says the reality of a lot of complex science topics is that they occur at scales we can't comprehend. "Whether its nanotechnology at a smaller scale or environmental science at a larger scale, these scales are not familiar to the general public. You can't see the whole ocean at once. Beyond our scale of perception you need visualization."

San Francisco's Exploratorium is "a museum of science, art and human perception"[15] designed to awaken visitors' curiosity. Tools and experiences, like explore-for-yourself exhibits, try to make learning, and understanding, playful and fun. Science centers are seen as a new way to explain complicated subjects. They are set up much like a laboratory, and museum visitors are encouraged to interact with hands-on exhibits for a learning experience that's intended to be visually engaging and tactile. "These are places where people can regain their confidence in science after they've finished school," observes the Exploratorium's executive director, Dennis Bartels. "They can come here to comprehend the world and ask questions of it. That's becoming harder and harder to do these days when you read about complicated things like the Higgs boson in the newspapers."

Visualizations help us see a broad range of topics like evolution, genomics, climate change, ocean currents, biotech, and material science in a new light. The Nanoscale Informal Science Education (NISE) Network created a "Viz Lab" at the Exploratorium in 2005 thanks to a grant from the National Science Foundation.[16] Its goal: to create a learning experience for people to experience what the nanoscale means in a way they can understand (see Figure 30.1).

Exploratorium visitors and people at other museums, libraries, and even university research centers experienced the subject of nano-technology in a way that a textbook or a lecture couldn't. Walk into the exhibit and see illustrations, "zooms," diagrams, and physical models that make the hard-to-imagine world of nanotechnology came to life. A variety of different visualization tools were used to make the difficult subject accessible at a more human scale:

▷ ILLUSTRATIONS. A series of illustrations showed familiar objects "across ten orders of magnitude." See the human blood stream, a butterfly wing, or a computer chip up close . . . real close. Make connections between objects from vast size scales.[17]

▷ ZOOMS. Let the audience see an object at a different scale. Zooms helped visitors go from what they saw in real life to a level where an object is beyond perception. They got a sense of relative size and understood that things are composed of smaller parts.[18]

▷ **DIAGRAMS.** Diagrams showed how objects were related by size, so museum-goers were able to quickly convey the size of the nanoscale.[19]

▷ **SIMULATIONS.** Visitors were provided with access to systems, objects, or phenomena that can't be manipulated, such as hurricanes, traffic patterns, and atomic behavior. They helped learners not just comprehend the object being studied, but its behavior.

▷ **PHYSICAL MODELS.** Hands-on and cost effective, these three-dimensional tangible representations of real-world or theoretical objects are a "particularly rich avenue for exploring the structure and geometry of the nanoscale in an informal setting."[20]

Figure 30-1 *Science centers, like the Exploratorium in San Francisco, offer unique opportunities to connect with complicated subjects in a manner that makes learning more tangible and experiential.*

Source: Amy Snyder, © Exploratorium, www.exploratorium.edu.

In a span of about 25 years, science centers grew from a handful to several hundred throughout the world. Innovations that engage people at an emotional level, like the Exploratorium's Viz Lab, have clearly helped their popularity. The power of experiential learning is on the rise.

People comprehend challenging content, claims Elsa Feher, when they can engage in active learning. The San Diego State University professor suggests that "mentally organizing the material into a coherent cognitive representation and mentally integrating the material with their existing knowledge"[21] is beneficial to learning. Science centers give students first-hand experience with natural phenomena, a good thing to counterbalance didactic teaching from the classroom. Science centers like the Exploratorium offer people the chance to explore new subjects in a welcoming venue.

It's good to mix things up; variety stimulates the mind. Mounted illustrations, simulations, physical models, and so on are some of the tools you can use to explain content. Multimedia gives you the chance to shake things up by providing your audience with different visuals, textures, sounds, even aromas . . . so their minds don't wander elsewhere. You'll keep your audience's attention longer if you offer them a variety of learning opportunities.[22] When they see "human advantages" to discoveries—their curiosity will be piqued. When they identify with the topic, their emotions will naturally kick in, thus enhancing their overall participation.[23]

You may not go out and build an entire museum with elaborate teaching exhibits, but may consider replicating some of the ideas coming from science centers in a scaled down manner. A hands-on or sensory display in your building's lobby or in a room adjacent to your conference may be a possibility. Think about trade shows and other types of exhibits. In a way, these events are a sort of commercialized science center. Vendors compete with each other to drive traffic to their booths. They entice potential customers with candy and giveaways with hopes they'll linger at the booth long enough to learn something about their products and services. Effective displays often take advantage of multimedia to communicate their message. The more interesting things the customers can see, touch, or interact with, the better.

You can also look for smaller opportunities to create a sensory experience for your audience. Can you reach them through visually dynamic means? Are there relevant products or materials you can let them touch or smell? Can you reproduce sounds or play music that will strike an emotional chord? Remember, humans respond to phenomenon that awakens their senses. This fosters learning and ultimately delivers meaning. Create a memorable experience for them, but remember—all good supercommunicator tools in moderation.

ARE GAMES AN EFFECTIVE TEACHING TOOL?

My only experience with an educational game was writing some of the content for NASA's "Station Spacewalk Game."[24] Players were tasked with repair work on the International Space Station to keep it operational. They had to perform designated jobs like installing an Integrated Truss Segment and unfurling a Solar Array before oxygen ran out. The game became popular. NASA considered it a success. At the very least, it helped engage a new generation in thinking about space exploration.

Starry-eyed educators would like to believe games are the next big thing in education. They see the explosive growth of the game industry as a sign that people will come to understand complicated topics via the Xbox equivalent of the day. Raised on computer-based games and simulations, Millennials, some argue, have different neurological requirements for learning.[25] Our new digital world demands highly interactive, media-intensive learning environments for them to flourish. Games, it seems, are the logical solution.

Not so fast, warn Finnish researchers Kristian Kiili and Harri Ketamo. Most game-based learning today is being done without significant pedagogical input. They say that most of what's disguised as educational games is a waste of time. They write that players aren't usually allowed to actively test their hypotheses and discover new knowledge with what's currently available.[26] The effective learning game encourages the player to develop their mental conceptual structure. But this won't be achieved until games that support reflective thinking are made available.[27]

There is more research that needs to be done about simulations and games. Most of our audiences will appreciate these tools for their novelty. But how much meaning do they bring? We haven't perfected the art of turning simulations and games into proven learning tools. When more adult learning experts collaborate with developers and produce pedagogically sound products, maybe we'll see a whole new field of education unfold. Until then, I would invest my money and effort in developing learning tools that do more than look cool.

31

Your Role as a
Supercommunicator

M ost citizens realize that since the September 11, 2001, terrorist
attacks security needed to be tightened, but the public is finding that the U.S. government's drastic espionage buildup is impacting
their personal liberties. An ongoing debate rages about the role of government on this emotionally charged subject.

For several years now, the media has been abuzz about how much
security is too much, not enough, or just right for the nation. In July
2010, *Washington Post* investigative reporter Dana Priest and columnist William M. Arkin published the product of two years putting
together a three-part series detailing what they call an unprecedented
buildup of national security. They left no stone unturned in their

reporting. Sorting through hundreds of thousands of public records, they identified 45 government agencies and 1,931 private companies that operate in what they call "Top Secret America."[28] Priest says this evolution is something that needs the public's attention. She believes most of us don't understand the magnitude of a national defense program that seems to be taking steroids, nor do we appreciate its potential consequences. "It's the size, the lack of transparency and the cost," she says, "and if we don't get it right, the consequences are gigantic."[29]

Priest wanted to tell the American people about the buildup in a way that would make them comprehend the extent of the situation. As an investigative reporter, her natural tool of the trade is the written word; journalists have always depended on text to explain news to their readers. But Priest knew words alone wouldn't provide a comprehensive picture of a story on this scale. Her readers needed to experience the enormity of the situation to understand why they should be concerned.

Working with a team of dozens, Priest and Arkin developed a multimedia experience that enabled *Post* readers to see data about the buildup in a way that transcended the written word. A large color wheel helped you explore the relationships between 45 government organizations and the type of work they do in fields like intelligence, the military, homeland security, and weapons technology (http://projects.washingtonpost.com/top-secret-america/network/). An interactive map, following a video introduction, allowed you to enter your geographic location to investigate what kind of security work is being done in your hometown (http://projects.washingtonpost.com/top-secret-america/map/). The *Post*'s use of these digital age features not only connected you to the larger story, but gave you a sense of the complexities of the nation's counterterrorism efforts.

Priest told me her graphic team's efforts "added something to the journalism . . . something that journalism could not bring to readers." With big data projects there's just too much data to organize in your head. She sees visualizations as a means to "deepen our journalism and not just make it fun." The *Post* put these applications online because the subject is "more graspable when you visualize it." Additionally, this Pulitzer Prize–winning journalist says the applications developed for "Top Secret America" helped her better comprehend the complexities of this subject so she could do a better job reporting.

The *Washington Post's* effort to help its readers visualize and experience the data in a new manner gives us a glimpse into our future as communicators. We can expect the role of graphics and applications to continue to expand in all of our communication efforts. Supercommunicator Priest wasn't shy about jumping on the visualization bandwagon. She comprehended the significance of the graphic image and the importance of tools that engage audiences, and acted. She didn't personally develop the applications, but she had a hand in working with her team to develop the tools needed to get the job done. Supercommunicators know that to be effective in today's digital age, they need to understand and embrace a new paradigm. They don't have to build the applications themselves, but they need to be an integral part of the discussion.

A ROLE FOR EVERYONE

How do you see your role evolving as a supercommunicator in the digital age? There are many paths you can take to incorporate multimedia/visualizations/infographics into your business. Minimally, it's important to understand how new digital tools are reshaping the way we communicate. By reading this book, you're well on your way. Being educated about how these tools can add value to your outreach efforts is essential. Keep learning as much as you can about this fascinating field.

Some people working with multimedia and visualizations don't do any of the actual building of the application or design, but collaborate with a team of specialists to produce the desired result. Dana Priest is an example of someone who supervises, but does not create visualizations. She functioned as the team captain or editor-in-chief in coordinating efforts to drive "Top Secret America."

Conversely, there are plenty of folks who are ready to roll up their sleeves and get busy. Many communicators are choosing to create their own visuals and applications. This model is favored by, but not limited to, Millennials—the generation who grew up using technology at an early age. Surprisingly, many of them don't have IT or design backgrounds, yet they are able to produce quality products. For many younger people, developing applications is like an extension of writing. You just go ahead and do it.

Many of us will fall somewhere between the hands-off executive and the hands-on, do-it-yourselfer. Some easier do-it-yourself applications are within our reach, but many of us will need to outsource larger projects to media and visualization professionals. Since immersing myself in this topic, I've come to appreciate the need for communicators to *feel* the data. With so many easy graphics programs available, it seems unnecessary at times to hire a designer when you can just use a template to do the job. Also, working hands-on gives you a more tactile experience with the numbers and visuals. This could lead to better communication.

Conversely, I am skeptical of people who don't know how to work with data suddenly having the tools to explain it to others. I learned from studying statistics that there are risks to playing with numbers when you don't fully understand them. As far as graphics go, I agree with John Grimwade that the world is filled with misleading visuals. Too many do-it-yourselfers can lead to a collective communication nightmare.

BE THE GLUE. BE THE EDITOR.

The more complicated the project, the more players will be involved. Someone needs to guide them and coordinate resources. The supercommunicator is the "glue" for a team of computer jockeys, designers, numbers people, and others. As the editor-in-chief, the supercommunicator keeps an eye on the big picture. Make sure that all the tasks being completed by others are ultimately going to produce a product that delivers meaning. Effective multimedia, visualizations, and infographics tell stories. With so many different parties working feverishly to get their jobs done, it's easy for them to lose focus.

Some supercommunicators, however, are highly adept in producing multimedia and visualizations. The NASA hyperwall project described in Chapter 3 was produced by a group of over a dozen people—all of them highly skilled in the art and science of creating visualizations. Horace Mitchell heads up the Scientific Visualization Studio (SVS) located at NASA's Goddard Space Flight Center. As director, he oversees the development of the dynamic graphics and videos produced there. He expects his team to be adept in the following areas:

▷ GOOD SENSE OF DESIGN AND AESTHETICS. Some team members have formal design training.

▷ SOLID IT SKILLS. All visualizers must be able to run and write sophisticated programs. Some team members come from an IT background.

▷ EFFECTIVE COMMUNICATIONS SKILLS/SCIENCE KNOWLEDGE. They must be able to converse with scientists and comprehend the subject matter.

▷ STRONG ANALYTICAL SKILLS. SVS visualizers must be able to work knowledgeably with data.

The task of finding a dozen people with these skill sets sounds incredibly difficult to me—but somehow Mitchell has succeeded in organizing such a group. Be mindful that there is this level of talent out there—you'll just have to work to find it.

JUST JUMP IN

As I was interviewing people about data visualizations, multimedia, and infographics, I wondered how easy it is for communicators not currently in the digital game to adopt some of these new ways. Surprisingly, I found out that creating visualizations isn't as epically difficult as one might imagine. Sure, the NASA example requires a team of incredibly qualified people, but some tools are easy enough for just about any of us to learn. According to Alberto Cairo of the University of Miami, "Anybody can learn about the visualization business in a couple of months."

The *teach yourself to do visualization* theory was popular among many of the professionals with whom I spoke. Liz Danzico, the chair of the Masters of Fine Arts Interaction Design program at the School of Visual Arts in New York, was among the many voices who said students need to "get into the culture, just jump in." Programs to help you produce visualizations are available online and some are relatively intuitive to learn.

ProPublica's Scott Klein is all about the do-it-yourself model of news applications. He says all of the news apps they produce are developed by journalists—people with liberal arts backgrounds, not IT or design. He says his hires have been highly trainable . . . able to learn how to work with searchable databases to tell a story. They have a good news and design sense, says Klein. "Teaching them the code is the easy part." Additionally, ProPublica pays for no specialty software. Everything it uses to create news apps is open source (computer software with a freely available source code).

Formal training in data visualization is still in its infancy. If you're thinking about asking a local college what visualization classes they teach . . . good luck. Offerings are slim in this new field. The School of Visual Arts, the University of Miami, and the University of North Carolina in Chapel Hill are options, but most educators I spoke to suggested prospective students start working with data and design by themselves before applying. Part of the challenge is that multidisciplinary nature of visualizations—drawing on design, programming, statistics, and journalism. It's hard to put all of that into a cohesive program.

Alberto Cairo offered me some great advice for individuals wanting to take the next step in this field. But first, let me recommend his book, *The Functional Art: An Introduction to Information Graphics and Visualization*, as a starting point. His book builds on many of the ideas presented in *Supercommunicator* and will give you more specific information about what it takes to excel.

Cairo recommends that infographic and visualization enthusiasts do these three things:

1. **READ TWO BOOKS AS PRIMERS:** *Show Me the Numbers* by Stephen Few and *White Space Is Not Your Enemy* by Kim Golombisky and Rebecca Hagen.

2. **START READING GRAPHICS CRITICALLY.** Pick up newspapers or go online and spend some time analyzing the graphic. Is it just a pretty image? Or does it tell a story? As you advance you'll also begin to see that sometimes data visualizers manipulate data—either on purpose to make a point, or because they are not as comfortable with data as they should be.

3. **GET STARTED.** Like Danzico advised, "just jump in." As you learn about information design, start producing graphics of your own. Work in Illustrator and Excel. Take a story that's filled with statistics—lots of numbers—and envision your design. Cairo recommends taking stories from *The New Yorker* because they often have data-intensive content.

A Debt of Gratitude

I am greatly appreciative of the many people who walked with me on the journey of writing this book.

A special callout goes to the folks who read my many drafts and offered support. They include: John McGaw, Eric Zakim, Steve Drake, Marie Deer, Denise Tortora, and Monica Cavanaugh.

Additionally, I would like to thank the many other contributors—people who welcomed me to interview them, offered helpful tips, or just listened to me as I blathered on about my project:

Robbin Ahrold

Gregor Aisch

Carole Al Kahouaji

Joseph P. Allen

Bill Amt

Ricardo Andrade

James Barrat

Tom Becker

Alexander Biles

Sheila Bjornstad

Robert Blinken Jr.

Danny Boice

Bruce Bradley

Rusty Burke

Alberto Cairo

John Cangany

Ben Carlson

Stephanie Cavanaugh

Vint Cerf

Connie Citro

Jarrett S. Cohen
Congressional Cemetery
   Dog Walkers
Peter Corbett
Kathy Cox
Patrick Crowley
Bill Cutter
Shana Dale
Liz Danzico
Marie Deer
Alex Demendonca
John Detrow
Gene Dixon
Mark Drapeau
Robert Draper
Andrew Dunn
Paul Dunning
Tom Dwyer
Pamela Ey
Anthony S. Fauci
James and Diane Fischer
Ira Flatow
Greg Folkers
Jen Frazier
Jason Fries
Daphne Frydman
Alex Glaros
Terry and Ann Goodwin
Eleanor Grant
Jeremy Greenfield
John Grimwade
Mary Ellen Hackett
Maggie Hall
Sabrina Horn
Noah Iliinsky
Paul Jensen
Peggy Jodry

Diane Johnson
Mark Kadesh
Kitty Kaupp
Alan Kelly
Randall Kelly
Timothy Kilbourn
Scott Klein
Karil Kochenderfer
Rami Koskinen
Tim Krebb
Jurgen Laartz
Jay Labov
Neil Lang
Bruce Lehman
Greg Linch
Andy Mannle
David McConville
Horace Mitchell
Peter Montgomery
Morning regulars @
   Peregrine Espresso
Sarah Orye
Matt Palumbo
Al and Brooke Pastro
David Pensak
Daniel Pink
Robert S. Pohl
Massimo Portincaso
Ben Prickril
Dana Priest
Bill Quain
Lee Rainie
Robert Reed
Deborah Reguera
Peter Reid
David Rejeski
James Reston Jr.

Rebecca Roberts
Jennifer Rosenberg
Louis Ross
Adam Rubinson
Michael P. Ryan
Matt Sadinsky
Dominic Sale
Rocky Sease
Peter and Marilu Sherer
Larry Slagle
Bruno Speck
Dennis Stanford
Ransom Stephens
Todd Stocke
Robert Stoll

Dan Tanglerini
Meinald Thielsch
Adrianne Threatt
John Tomczyk
Guilio de Tommaso
Suzanne Turner
Kathleen Vogel
Trent Waterhouse
William Wattie
Steven Weinberg
Joyce C. West
Susanne Westermann
Diane Yameogo
Michael Zimbalist

Notes

INTRODUCTION

1. John L. Beckley, *The Power of Little Words* (Fairfield, NJ: The Economics Press, 1984), p. 128.

PART I: HOW DIGITAL TECHNOLOGY IS CHANGING COMMUNICATION

1. Brian Greene, "The God Particle," Aspen Ideas Festival, http://www. aspenideas.org/session/god-particle. Retrieved August 7, 2012.
2. Marc Prensky, "Digital Natives, Digital Immigrants," *On the Horizon*, vol. 9, no. 5 (2001).
3. "Millennials: Confident, Connected and Open to Change." Pew Research Social and Demographic Trends (February 24, 2010). Retrieved August 8, 2013 from http://www.pewsocialtrends.org/2010/02/24/millennials-confident- connected-open-to-change/.
4. Nicholas Carr, *The Shallows: What the Internet Is Doing to Our Brains* (New York: Norton, 2011), p. 10.
5. Glen Bull, et al., "Connecting Informal and Formal Learning Experiences in the Age of Participatory Media," *CITE*, vol. 8, no. 2 (2008). Retrieved October 17, 2013 from http://www.citejournal.org/vol8/iss2/editorial/article1.cfm.

6. "Scientists' Strategic Reading Enhanced by Digital Tools," *Mathematics and Economics* (August 18, 2009).

7. Pew Research Center's Internet & American Life Project, "How Teens Do Research in the Digital World" (November 1, 2012).

8. "The 2013 Pulitzer Prize Winners, Feature Writing," http://www.pulitzer. org/citation/2013-Feature-Writing.

9. Robert Frederick, "How 'Snow Fall' Transforms Journalism," *National Association of Science Writers* (April 28, 2013), https://www.nasw.org/ how-snow-fall-transforms-journalism.

10. Jeremy Rue, "The Snowfall Effect and Dissecting the Multimedia Longform Narrative," http://multimediashooter.com/wp/2013/04/21/the-snow-fall-effect-and-dissecting-the-multimedia-longform-narrative/. ·

11. RSA Animate, http://www.thersa.org/events/rsaanimate.

12. Dan Kusnetzky, "What Is Big Data?" *ZDNet* (February 16, 2010), http:// www.zdnet.com/blog/virtualization/what-is-big-data/1708.

13. Vivek Kundra, "Digital Fuel of the 21st Century: Innovation through Open Data and the Network Effect." Joan Shorenstein Center, Harvard University, John F. Kennedy School of Government, January 2012, p. 5.

14. "E-Book Reading Jumps . . ." Pew Research Center's Internet & American Life Project, December 27, 2012. As of November 2012, some 25 percent of Americans ages 16 and older own tablet computers such as iPads or Kindle Fires, up from 10 percent who owned tablets in late 2011.

15. Edward Tufte, "The Cognitive Style of PowerPoint: Pitching Out Corrupts Within," in *Beautiful Evidence* (Cheshire, CT: Graphics Press LLC, 2006), pp. 155–185.

16. Ibid., p. 184.

17. Ibid., p. 160.

18. Ibid., p. 184.

19. M. T. Thielsch and I. Perabo, "Use and Evaluation of Presentation Software," *Technical Communication*, vol. 59, no. 2 (2012), pp. 112–123.

20. Craig Timberg and Jialynn Yang, "Bezos's Management Philosophy: Two Pizzas not Three," *The Washington Post* (August 8, 2013).

PART II: KNOW THY AUDIENCE

1. Asynchronous Transfer Mode (ATM) is "a high-speed networking standard designed to support both voice and data communications. ATM is normally utilized by Internet service providers on their private long-distance networks." Bradley Mitchell, About.com Guide.

2. The term "Information Superhighway" was widely used to refer to the

Internet telecommunications network before use of the Internet became widespread.

3. Jay B. Labov and Barbara Kline Pope, "Understanding Our Audiences: The Design and Evolution of *Science, Evolution, and Creationism.*" *CBE Life Sciences Education,* vol. 7, no. 1 (Spring 2008), pp. 20–24.

4. National Academy of Sciences and Institute of Medicine, *Science, Evolution, and Creationism* (Washington, DC: The National Academies Press, 2008), p. 32.

5. Dennis J. Stanford and Bruce A. Bradley, *Across Atlantic Ice: The Origin of America's Clovis Culture* (Berkeley: University of California Press, 2012), p. 241.

PART III: KNOW THY SUBJECT

1. The book *Elite and Specialized Interviewing* by Lewis A. Dexter (New York: Columbia University Press, 2008) offers tips helpful to interviewing professionals.

2. The pen/pad tool I use is called "Livescribe."

PART IV: SIMPLICITY AND CLARITY

1. "Simplicity," http://www.merriam-webster.com/dictionary/simplicity.

2. "Clarity," http://dictionary.reference.com/browse/clarity.

3. Henry David Thoreau. *Walden and Other Writings.* http://www.goodreads.com/work/quotes/6755636.

4. Ney, D. E., *American Technological Sublime* (Cambridge, MA: MIT Press, 1994), p. 57, cited in *The Techno-Human Condition* by Braden R. Allenby and Daniel Sarewitz (Cambridge, MA: MIT Press, 2011).

5. According to Flatow, with podcast listeners, that number jumps to 2 million listeners per week.

6. Ira Flatow, *Present at the Future* (New York: HarperCollins, 2007), p. 155.

7. Ibid., p. 159.

8. John Medina, *Brain Rules: 12 Principles for Surviving and Thriving at Work, Home, and School* (Seattle, WA: Pear Press, 2008).

9. V. G. Cerf, "The Day the Internet Age Began," *Nature,* vol. 461, no. 7268 (2009), pp. 1202–1203.

10. Paul Laudicina, *Beating the Global Odds* (New York: Wiley, 2012), p. 82.

11. Ibid., p. 86.

12. US Patent and Trademark Office, "U.S. Patent Statistics Chart, Calendar Years 1963–2012," http://www.uspto.gov/web/offices/ac/ido/oeip/taf/us_stat.htm.
13. The USPTO does not track or measure the actual number of patents returned for this reason.

PART V: GUIDELINES FOR EFFECTIVE COMMUNICATION

1. Bill Welch, ed., *The Analyst's Style Manual* (Erie, PA: Mercyhurst College Institute for Intelligence Studies Press, 2008). http://www.ncirc.gov/documents%5Cpublic%5Canalysts_style_manual.pdf.
2. "Theoria," http://shelf3d.com/i/theoria.
3. John L. Beckley, *The Power of Little Words* (Fairfield, NJ: The Economics Press, 1984), p. 27.
4. Jonathan Guthrie, "Three Cheers for the Epic Poetry of Jargon," *Financial Times* (December 13, 2007).
5. Ibid.

PART VI: HUMANIZE YOUR COMMUNICATIONS

1. Carmine Gallo, *The Presentation Secrets of Steve Jobs: How to Be Insanely Great in Front of Any Audience* (New York: McGraw-Hill, 2010).
2. Ruth Colvin Clark and Richard E. Mayer, *e-Learning and the Science of Instruction: Proven Guidelines for Consumers and Designers of Multimedia Learning* (San Francisco: Pfeiffer, 2008), p. 173.
3. Ibid., pp. 168–173.
4. *The Janz Awakening*. Ryder Integrated Logistics, 1997, Preface.
5. Muriel Rukeyser, "The Speed of Darkness," from *The Collected Poems of Muriel Rukeyser*. Copyright © 2006 by Muriel Rukeyser. Reprinted by permission of International Creative Management, 1968.
6. Meera Lee Sethi and Adam Briggle, "Making Stories Visible: The Task for Bioethics Commissions," *Issues in Science and Technology* (Winter 2011).
7. M. Carolyn Clark and Marsha Rossiter, *Narrative Learning in Adulthood* (Malabar, FL: Krieger Publishing Company, 2007), p. 65.
8. Sharan B. Merriam and Rosemary S. Caffarella, *Learning in Adulthood: A Comprehensive Guide,* 3rd ed. (San Francisco: Jossey-Bass, 2007), p. 223.
9. Daniel Yergin and Joseph Stanislaw, *The Commanding Heights: The Battle for the World Economy* (New York: Simon & Schuster/Touchtone, 1998).

10. David R. Henderson, "How the Markets Beat Marx," *Fortune*, August 3, 1998. Retrieved October 15, 2013, from http://money.cnn.com/magazines/fortune/fortune_archive/1998/08/03/246274/index.htm
11. Paul Smith, *Lead with a Story* (New York: AMACOM, 2012), p. 119.
12. Alice LaPlante, *The Making of a Story* (New York: W.W. Norton Company, 2007), p. 155.
13. GS&C founder John Sperling coined this phrase, according to Carlson.
14. Bertrand Moullier and Michael P. Ryan, "A Picture Is Worth . . . Bollywood Battles the Movie Pirates with Law and Tech," *IP Supplement to Legal Times* (July 23, 2007).
15. http://cis-india.org/a2k/blog/piracy-studies-india. Retrieved on July 22, 2013.
16. Moullier and Ryan.
17. Victoria J. Marsick, "Case Study," in *Adult Learning Methods*, ed. Michael W. Galbraith (Malabar, FL: Krieger Publishing, 2003), p. 229.
18. Ibid., p. 230.
19. Ibid., p. 230.
20. Clark and Mayer, pp. 162–165.
21. "Special Stylistic Issues in Technical Writing," https://www.e-education.psu.edu/styleforstudents/c1_p15.html. Retrieved on July 1, 2013.
22. Ann Handley and C.C. Chapman, *Content Rules: How to Create Killer Blogs, Podcasts, Videos, Ebooks and Webinars (and more) that Engage Your Customers and Ignite Your Business* (Hoboken, NJ: Wiley, 2012), p. 171.

PART VII: GETTING AN AUDIENCE TO CARE

1. John Medina, *Brain Rules: 12 Principles for Surviving and Thriving at Work, Home, and School* (Seattle, WA: Pear Press, 2008) p. 82..
2. Hanna Trudo and Theodoric Meyer, "Dollars for Docs: The Top Earners," *ProPublica* (March 12, 2013), http://www.propublica.org/article/dollars-for-docs-the-top-earners.
3. "About Us," *ProPublica,* http://www.propublica.org/about/.
4. Samuel Weigley, "AT&T, T-Mobile Merger: A Timeline of Events in the Wireless Debate," *International Business Times* (November 26, 2011), http://www.ibtimes.com/att-t-mobile-merger-timeline-events-wireless-debate-374994.
5. "AT&T Ends Bid to Add Network Capacity through T-Mobile USA Purchase," AT&T Press Release (December 19, 2011), http://www.att.com/gen/press-room?pid=22146&cdvn=news&newsarticleid=33560.
6. Raymond J. Wlodkowski, "Strategies to Enhance Adult Motivation to

Learn," in *Adult Learning Methods,* ed. Michael W. Galbraith (Malabar, FL: Krieger Publishing, 1990), p. 113.

7. Drew Westen, *The Political Brain: The Role of Emotion in Deciding the Fate of the Nation* (New York: Perseus Books Group, 2007).

PART VIII: BUILDING BLOCK AND ANALOGIES

1. Ruth Colvin Clark and Richard E. Mayer, *e-Learning and the Science of Instruction: Proven Guidelines for Consumers and Designers of Multimedia Learning* (San Francisco: Pfeiffer, 2008), p. 39.

2. Kathleen Taylor and Annalee Lamoreaux, "Teaching with the Brain in Mind," in *Update on Adult Learning Theory,* 3rd ed., ed. Sharan B. Merriam (Hoboken, NJ: 2008).

3. Ibid.

4. I transcribed this passage from the DVD "Amazing Planet," *National Geographic* (2007).

5. The architects also currently hold the chair of Architecture and Urban Design at the ETH Zurich.

PART IX: VISUAL AND INTERACTIVE

1. John Medina, *Brain Rules: 12 Principles for Surviving and Thriving at Work, Home, and School* (Seattle, WA: Pear Press, 2008) p. 240.

2. Ibid., p. 234.

3. Ruth Colvin Clark and Richard E. Mayer, *e-Learning and the Science of Instruction: Proven Guidelines for Consumers and Designers of Multimedia Learning* (San Francisco: Pfeiffer, 2008), pp. 53-73.

4. 3D-Forensic, Seek and Illustrate the Truth, http://www.3d-forensic.com/?tag=jason-c.

5. Ruth Clark, "Give Your Training a Visual Boost," *T+D* (April 2009), p. 36.

6. Alberto Cairo, "The Functional Art," *New Riders* (2013), p. xxi.

7. Edward Tufte, "The Cognitive Style of PowerPoint: Pitching Out Corrupts Within," in *Beautiful Evidence* (Cheshire CT: Graphics Press, LLC), p. 107.

8. Clark, "Give Your Training a Visual Boost," p. 36.

9. Amy Balliett, "The Do's and Dont's of Infographic Design," *Smashing Magazine* (October 14, 2011), http://www.smashingmagazine.com/2011/10/14/the-dos-and-donts-of-infographic-design/. Retrieved March 26, 2013.

10. Dr. Fauci's full presentation with comments are available at Anthony Fauci, "Thirty Years of HIV/AIDS: A Scientific Journey and Look to the Future," 6th IAS Conference on HIV Pathogenesis, Treatment and Prevention, Rome, Italy, July 17–20, 2011, http://pag.ias2011.org/flash.aspx?pid=409.

11. Tufte, pp. 157–185.

12. Tufte, p. 162.

13. Rachel Arandilla, "Presentation Tools: Keynote versus PowerPoint," 1st Web Designer Blog (2011), http://www.1stwebdesigner.com/design/keynote-vs-powerpoint/. Retrieved August 30, 2013.

14. "Meet Some Staff Scientists," Exploratorium, http://www.exploratorium.edu/about/staff-scientists. Retrieved July 10, 2013.

15. "About Us," Exploratorium, http://www.exploratorium.edu/about/staff-scientists. Retrieved July 10, 2013.

16. The NISE Network Viz Lab project ran from 2005 to 2009.

17. "Viz Lab Illustration," NISE Network, http://www.nisenet.org/viz_lab/illustrations. Retrieved July 10, 2013.

18. Ibid.

19. Ibid.

20. Ibid.

21. Elsa Feher, "Interactive Museum Exhibits as Tools for Learning: Explorations with Light," *International Journal of Science Education*, vol. 12, no. 1 (1990), pp. 35–49.

22. Raymond J. Wlodkowski, "Strategies to Enhance Adult Motivation to Learn," in *Adult Learning Methods,* ed. Michael W. Galbraith (Malabar, FL: Krieger Publishing, 1990), p. 113.

23. Ibid., p. 114.

24. http://www.nasa.gov/multimedia/3d_resources/station_spacewalk_game.html.

25. Clark and Mayer, p. 347.

26. Kristian Kiili and Harri Ketamo, "Exploring the Learning Mechanism in Educational Games," *Journal of Computing and Information Technology*, Tampere University of Technology, Pori, Finland, vol. 4 (CIT 15, 2007), pp. 319–324.

27. Ibid., p. 319.

28. Dana Priest and William Arkin, "Top Secret America: A Washington Post Investigation," *The Washington Post,* http://projects.washingtonpost.com/top-secret-america/articles/methodology/. Retrieved June 22, 2013; Dana Priest and William Arkin, *Top Secret America: The Rise of the New American Security* (New York: Little, Brown and Company, 2011).

29. Priest and Arkin, "Top Secret America."

Index

acronyms, 80, 114–115

Across Atlantic Ice (Stanford and Bradley), 66–67

active voice, 106

Al-Kahouaji, Carole, 22

Allen, Joseph P., 53

Allen, Robbie, 151–152

Amazing Planet, 182

Amazon
  Kindle, 41–42
  narratives at, 45

Amazon Web Service, 159

American Archaeology, 67

analogies, 168, 188
  aha moments, 179–180
  brain and, 180–181
  misconception from, 183
  in professional setting, 185–189
  Star Trek, 177–179

Analyst's Style Manual, 105–106

animal cloning, 141–143

animation, 29, 136, 196–197, 208

AP Style Manual, 106

APCO Online, 161

Apollo 13 crisis, 53–54

apology for storytelling, 139

Arandilla, Rachel, 217

Arkin, William M., 225–227

art, vs. visualizations, 202, 205

artificial intelligence, 151

Arvai, Peter, 217

Aspen Ideas Festival, 16

Asynchronous Transfer Mode (ATM), 49–50, 238*n1*

AT&T, 161–163

Athens Olympics, 202, 203

audiences
  addressing multiple, 65–74
  analogies for, 181
  avoiding insults of, 98–99
  awareness in small to mid-sized, 60–63
  awareness of, 49–51, 154
  cultural awareness of, 71
  details and, 93
  engagement, personality and, 122
  familiar items for, 183–184
  getting them to care, 155–156

audiences *(continued)*
    infographics to gain attention,
        31
    information relevance to, 159
    misreading, 53–56
    multimedia best fit for, 45–47
    research on, 57–63
    skepticism of, 164
    synchronizing content with
        culture, 116–117
audio, 27–28, 135–136
auditing standards, 90
auditory learning, vs. visual, 193
Automated Insights, 151
avalanches, *New York Times* on,
    26–27
awareness
    cultural, of audience, 71
    in small to mid-sized audiences,
        60–63

background information, for writers,
    85
Balliett, Amy, 31, 208
Bandit Queen, 147
Barrat, James, *Our Final Invention*,
    151
Bartels, Dennis, 220
Beating the Global Odds (Laudicina),
    99
Beautiful Evidence (Tufte), 214
Becker, Tom, 11–12
Beckley, John L., 3
    The Power of Little Words, 112
Bedi, Bobby, 146–147
Berlitz International, 159
best practices, 2
best-selling business books, 152
Bezos, Jeff, 45
bidirectional dialogue, 38
big data
    humanizing, 152
    visualization, 33–34

biological weapons threats, knowl-
    edge about, 68–69
Bloomberg Businessweek, 119
books, 21
    vs. web page information, 37
Boston Consulting Group, 40
box chart, 94
Bradley, Bruce, 65–67
bragging, 152
brain
    analogies and, 180–181
    patterns and, 172
    rewiring by Internet, 20–22
    visual stimuli processing by, 193
Brain Rules (Medina), 193
brevity, 89, 115
Brillembourg, Alfredo, 186
broadcast media, vs. dialogue, 40
budget requests, analogy limitations
    in, 187
building blocks, 167–168, 170, 172
bullet points, 216
Burke, Rusty, 111
business books, best-selling, 152
business communication, video clips
    in, 28

Cairo, Alberto, 32–33, 230
    The Functional Art, 197–199, 231
Cangany, John, 161
Cannes Film Festival, 147
Caracas, Venezuela, housing
    projects, 186
Carlson, Ben, 142
Carlson, Tim, 26
Carr, Nicholas, 21
case examples, 145–149
case studies, tips for using, 148
casual tone, 153
Center for Digital Information, 19
Cerf, Vint, 97–98
change, 3
    resistance to, 89

chapters, length of, 115–116
charts, 28
    form and effectiveness of, 31–32
Chautauqua Institution, 11–12
Chicago Manual of Style, 106
clarity, 87, 89–90, 101–103, 123
    simplicity vs., 90
    and success, 5
Clark, Carolyn, 133–134
Clark, Ruth Colvin, 171, 199, 207
climax in story, 138
cloning pets, 141
cloud computing, 215
Cohen, Jarrett, 34
color, in images, 208
Colson, Charles, 76
comfort zone, 89
The Commanding Heights: The Battle for the World Economy (Yergin), 134
Common Craft, 29
communications
    digital, 1–6, 89
    guidelines for effective, 105–107
    multiple product route for, 68–69
companies, human face for, 128
comparison, 168, 177–184, 188, *see also* analogies
complexity, 2, 170
    layering to breakdown, 171–172
complication, avoiding, 88
comprehension, simplicity and, 88
conclusion, report beginning with, 109–110
Condé Nast Traveler, 201, 203
confidence, 77
Conflict-Crisis-Resolution Model, 138
consumption of electricity, and generation, 169–170
content
    efforts to explain complicated, 1–2
    making more human, 122–123

content experts, 80, 83–85
cooperative work, 191–192
copyrights, 146
corporate culture, blending into, 121
costs, of audience research, 61
COULOURlovers, 208
credibility, 79, 81, 164
criminal trial, 195–197
cultural differences, 116–117
cultural issues, research on, 71–74
cybersecurity, 165–166

Danzico, Liz, 230
DARPA (U.S. Department of Defense Advanced Research Projects Agency), 98
data, on security buildup, 226
democratization of information, 3
Dench, Judi, 124–125
details
    leaving out, 93
    in storytelling, 139
developing economies, intellectual property and, 146
diagrams, 221
dialogue, 62
    vs. broadcast media, 40
Digital Book World, 41
digital communication, 1–6
    simplicity and, 89
digital media, 118
    characteristics, 38
    communication change from, 7–9
    need to learn, 22
digital natives, 20, 22, 120
    credibility and, 164
    information delivery preferences, 38, 39, 40
directness, 116
distraction, multimedia as, 137, 207

documents
  format and formality of, 154,
    187
  introduction, 109–110
  readability, 103, 115
  static, 19
Dodd-Frank Wall Street Reform
  and Consumer Protection
  Act, 94
do-it-yourselfers, for visuals
  creation, 228
Dollars for Docs, 157–158
drama, in case examples, 148
dynamic media, vs. static, 38–39

e-books, enhanced, 41
economics, storytelling on, 134–135
editor, supercommunicator as,
  228–229
ego, 55
ego-driven behavior, 152
Einstein, Albert, 77, 97
electricity
  analogies for, 188–189
  generation and consumption,
    169–170
electronic pen, 80, 239n2
Elo Touch Solutions, 70-inch
  screens, 218
emotions
  in U.S. politics, 163
  when to use, 165–166
empathy, 173
entry points for media, defined vs.
  multiple, 39
errors, avoiding, 117
ethics of doctors, 158
evolution, 58–59
experiencing information, 37–42,
  193
experiential learning, 222
Ey, Pamela, 170, 188

Facebook, 62
false statements, 77
Fauci, Anthony S., 51, 209
Federal Communications Commis-
  sion (FCC), 162
feedback, from specialists, 81
Feher, Elsa, 222
Few, Stephen, *Show Me the Numbers*,
  231
finding human voice, 121–125
first-person language, 121, 124
flaked stone technology, 67
Flatow, Ira, 91–92
  Present at the Future, 92
Flesch-Kincaid Grade Level, 103
food analogies, 71–72
formality
  of third person, 124
  in writing, 153–154
Frazier, Jennifer, 219
Freitag triangle, 138
Fries, Jason, 196, 205
Frost, David, 75–76
Frost/Nixon (film), 76
The Functional Art (Cairo), 197–199,
  231

Gallo, Carmine, 119–120
games, teaching with, 223–224
Gates, Bill, 119–120
Geek-Speak, vs. layman's language,
  4
generation of electricity, and
  consumption, 169–170
Genetic Savings & Clone, 141
genuineness, 123
global audience, communication
  style for, 116
The Goal (Goldratt), 132
Goldratt, Eliyahu, *The Goal*, 132
Golombisky, Kim, *White Space Is Not
  Your Enemy*, 231

Goodwin, Terry, 131
Google, 81
  Android operating system,
    128–129
  Presentation, 217
grammar, 102, 117
Grant, Eleanor, 181–182
graphic design, 191–194
  guidelines, 205–208
graphics, 28
  analyzing, 231
  quality of, 212–213
  risk of distorting statistics,
    206–207
graphs, 28
  form and effectiveness of, 31–32
Greene, Brian, 15–16
Greenfield, Jeremy, 41
Grimwake, John, 201–202, 203
guidelines, vs. rules, 106
Guthrie, Jonathan, 113

hackers, 165–166
Hagen, Rebecca, *White Space Is Not
    Your Enemy*, 231
hands-on learning experiences, 193
Hermes, 4
Higgs Boson case, 14–17
history, audience awareness of, 74
HIV/AIDS, history, 209–214
human experience, shared, 73
human voice
  finding, 121–125
  speaking with, without human,
    127–129
humanity, lesson in, 124–125

Iliinsky, Noah, 34
images, 28
  color in, 208
  PowerPoint for displaying, 216
  in storytelling, 136

Impress, 217
India
  cell phones in, 88
  illegal DVD copying, 147
individualism, 1980s perspective on,
    121
infographics, 2–3, 30–31
  impact of, 36
information
  access to, 12
  analyzing and sharing options,
    13
  democratization of, 3
  experiencing, 37–42, 193
  frameworks for, 13
  gathering about audience, 61
  holding back, 76
  overload, 54
  relevance to audiences, 159
  repackaging, 46
  sharing, 8
  static means of acquiring, 21
  winnowing process, 94–95
information hunters, vs. readers, 21
information smog, 99
Information Superhighway, 50,
    238n2
information technology architecture,
    conference on, 185–187
instant gratification, 22
Institute of Medicine, 58
integrity, 90
intellectual property rights, 145
intelligence (mental abilities), 120
intelligence gathering, weaknesses
    in, 69
interactive media, 40
  vs. static, 38–39
International AIDS Society (IAS)
    Conference on HIV Patho-
    genesis Treatment and
    Prevention, 209–214

Internet, 3, 89, 110
    for audience research, 61–62
    brains rewired by, 20–22
    communication style change
        from, 37
    as delivery mechanism, 19
    development, 50, 97–98
    impact on content, 120
    new outlets, 20
Internet firewall, 177
Internet Protocol (IP), 178
intrinsic motivation, 163
introduction of document, 109–110

The Janz Awakening, 132
jargon, 80, 102
    abuse of, 112–114
Jobs, Steve, 119–120
Johnson O'Connor Research
        Foundation, 111
jokes, 137
journal articles, networked, 21
Journal of Field Archaeology, 67
judgment, use of, 5–6

Kahn, Bob, 98
Ketamo, Harri, 223–224
Keynote, 217
Kiili, Kristian, 223–224
Kilbourn, Tim, 105–106
Killer Infographics, 31
Klein, Scott, 158, 230
Klumpner, Hubert, 186
knowledge, 3
    audience need for prerequisite,
        171–172
Krantz, Gene, 53–54
Kuler, 208
Kundra, Vivek, 40

Laartz, Jürgen, 186
Labov, Jay, 57–58
Lamoreaux, Annalee, 172, 180–181

language
    ease of understanding, 2
    first-person, 121, 124
    of specialists, 55, 80, 102, 113
Laudicina, Paul, *Beating the Global
        Odds*, 99
lava, 182
layering, 167–168, 170–171
    communications tips for,
        172–173
    for complexity breakdown,
        171–172
    movies for examples, 173–175
Lead with a Story (Smith), 103, 135
learning
    auditory vs. visual, 193
    case examples for, 145–149
    storytelling and, 133–134
legacy infrastructure issues, 186–187
libraries, 21
life, questions about diversity, 58–59
linear media, vs. nonlinear, 39
LinkedIn, 62
listening, to self, 123
Livescribe, 239n2
Lotus Symphony, 217

managers, identifying employee
        shortcomings in communica-
        tion, 56
maple syrup, 71
market research, for corporations, 61
Maya, 197
Mayer, Richard, 171
McKinsey & Company, 185
meaning
    delivery of, 11–17
    failure to deliver, 14
mechanized writing, 151
media
    broadcast vs. dialogue, 40
    defined vs. multiple entry points,
        39

linear vs. nonlinear, 39
opaque vs. transparent, 40
static vs. interactive/dynamic,
    38–39
text-heavy vs. visual, 39
Medina, John, 193
mental images, 71, 180
metaphors, 180
Microsoft Word, 103
Millennials, 20
misconception, from analogies,
    183
misinformation, 77
Mitchell, Horace, 229
motivation
    intrinsic, 163
    stories for, 135
movies, for layering examples,
    173–175
multimedia, 7, 14
    basics, 25–36
    best fit for audience, 45–47
    as distraction, 137, 205
    guidelines, 118, 205–208
    for learning, 222
    meaning of, 2
    quality, 197–199
    for storytelling, 135
    strategic use, 199
    user engagement with, 8
multimedia age, beginnings, 19–23

Nanoscale Informal Science
    Education (NISE) Network,
    220
nanotechnology, 92, 220
narratives, 45
NASA, 2, 154, 215
    acronym use, 114
    Center for Climate Simulation
        supercomputer, 34–35
    Goddard Space Flight Center,
        229
    reports on *Columbia*, 44
    Station Spacewalk Game, 223
National Academy of Sciences, 58
National Geographic Channel,
    181–182
National Institute of Allergy and
    Infectious Diseases (NIAID),
    51
National Science Foundation, 220
NetJets, 160
networked journal articles, 21
neuroplasticity, 20
New York Times, 25–26, 103, 198
    multimedia features, 26–27
news organizations, 25
Nigeria, Nollywood community, 147
Nixon, Richard, 75–76
nonlinear books, navigating, 41

omnibus survey, 61
opaque media, vs. transparent, 40
Orzel, Chad, 127
Our Final Invention (Barrat), 151
oversimplification, 97–99

Pankey, Ron, 26
paper documents, 8
paragraphs, length of, 103, 115–116
passive voice, 106
patents, 146
    delays from communication
        problems, 101
pedagogical agents, 129
Pensak, David, 177
personal computer, invention impact,
    192
personal details, 152–153, 211–212
personality, and audience engage-
    ment, 122
personalization, 157–160
pet cloning, 141
Pew Research Center, Internet &
    American Life Project, 23, 35

pharmaceutical companies, doctors' payments from, 157
photography, 28, 211–212
in storytelling, 136
physical models, 221
pictures, 193
Pietrucha, Frank A., 191
Pink, Daniel, 29
To Sell Is Human, 152–153
piracy, of intellectual property, 146
The Political Brain (Westen), 163
popular culture, 73
popular writing style, balancing with scientific style, 66–67
Portincaso, Massimo, 40
The Power of Little Words (Beckley), 112
power scanning, 21
PowerPoint, 43–45
alternatives, 216–217
decision to use, 214–215
tips for using, 216
Prehistoric American, 67
Prensky, Marc, 20
prerequisite knowledge, audience need for, 171–172
Present at the Future (Flatow), 92
presentations, 120
touch-screen technology for, 218
visuals for, 209–218
Prezi, 217
Priest, Dana, 158, 206, 225–227
print-based media, characteristics, 38
privacy issues, 62
professional communicator, working with, 84
professional setting, analogies in, 185–189
professionalism, 121
storytelling benefits, 133
Progressive Insurance, 128
ProPublica, 157–158, 230

public speaking, 84
pumpkin graphics, 207

quantum mechanics, 16

Rai, Vinay, 87–88, 117
Rainie, Lee, 22–23, 35
rational thinking, 161–168
readability of writing, 103, 115
readers, vs. information hunters, 21
Reid, Peter, 45
Rejeski, David, 133
reports, conclusion at beginning, 109–110
research on cultural issues, 71–74
resistance, to information system, overcoming, 131–132
resolution in story, 138
respect for audience, 98–99
Reston, James Jr., 75
Roberts, Rebecca, 71
Robinson, Sir Ken, 29
robots, writing by, 151
Rossiter, Marsha, 134
Royal Society for the Encouragement of Arts, Manufactures and Commerce (RSA), 29
Rukeyser, Muriel, 133
rules, vs. guidelines, 106
Ryan, Mike, 146
Ryder Logistics, 131–132

San Francisco, Exploratorium, 219–220
Saugstad, Elyse, 27
Schall, Joe, 153
Scherman Kent School for Intelligence Analysis, 105
scholarly writing, 153
School of Visual Arts, 230
Schwarzenegger, Arnold, 174
Science, Evolution, and Creationism, 58

science centers, 222
Science Friday, 91
science topics, scales for, 219
scientific style, balancing with
    popular writing style, 66–67
Scientific Visualization Studio
    (SVS), 229
Sease, Rocky, 170, 188
security, 225
sentences, length of, 115–116
shared experience, with audience,
    73–74
Show Me the Numbers (Few), 231
similies, 180
simplicity, 87–89
    clarity vs., 90
    in visuals, 206
simplifying, 91–95
    oversimplification, 97–99
simulations, 221
The 6th Day (film), 174
skepticism, of audience, 164
skill set, incorporating new features,
    4
Smith, Paul, 214
    Lead with a Story, 103, 135
social media, 62
    impact of, 118
Sourcebooks, Shakespeare series, 41
"speak human" style, 152
specialists
    communication problems, 13, 55
    exposure to outsiders, 56
    feedback from, 81
    guidelines for engaging with,
        81–82
    jargon and, 80, 102, 112–114
spell check, 117
sports, as shared experience, 74
Sprint, 162
stakeholder analysis template, 95
Stanford, Dennis, 65–67
Stanger, Jeff, 19

Star Trek, and firewall explanation,
    177–179
startups, message to investors, 2
static documents, 19
static media, vs. interactive/dynamic,
    38–39
statistical graphics, risk of distortion,
    206–207
stimulation, 20
Stocke, Todd, 41
Stoll, Bob, 101
stop-action animation videos, 29
storytelling, 110, 123, 128–129,
    131–139
    on economics, 134–135
    getting started with, 137–139
    and learning, 133–134
    multimedia for, 135
    stages, 138
    value of, 132
strategic plans, analogy limitations
    in, 187
style guides, 106
    for multimedia, 118
subject knowledge, 75–78
    lack of expertise, 79–82
subjectivity, 107
success, message clarity and, 5
supercommunicator, 4
    as editor, 228–229
    role as, 225–227
supercommunicator basic guidelines,
    109–118
    conclusion at report beginning,
        109–110
    error-free writing, 117
    on jargon, 112–114
    minimizing big words, 111–112
    sentence, paragraph, and chapter
        length, 115–116
    synchronizing content with
        audience culture, 116–117
survey design, 61

Taylor, Kathleen, 172, 180–181
teaching, with games, 223–224
technical discussion, 50
technical security policy, knowledge
    on, 68–69
technical topics, ease of understand-
    ing, 3
technical writers, 84
technology, Chautauqua Institution
    upgrades, 12
testimonials, 141–144
    case examples vs., 148–149
text-heavy media
    reducing in PowerPoint, 216
    vs. visual, 39
thinking, rational, 161–168
third person, 124, 154
Thoreau, Henry David, 88–89
Threatt, Adrianne, 94
3D Studio Max, 197
timeline matrix, for HIV/AIDS,
    210–211
T-Mobile USA, 161–163
To Sell Is Human (Pink), 152–153
"Top Secret America," 226–227
touch-screen technology, for
    presentations, 218
Toyota Prius, 160
trade shows, 222
trademarks, 146
training, in data visualization, 230
Transmission Control Protocol
    (TCP), 178
transparency, 82
transparent media, vs. opaque,
    40
Tufte, Edward, 43–44, 206
    Beautiful Evidence, 214
Turner, Suzanne, 141
Twitter, 62, 89

United States, emotions and politics,
    163

United States-India Business
    Council (USIBC), 147
U.S. Central Intelligence Agency,
    105
U.S. Department of Defense
    Advanced Research Projects
    Agency (DARPA), 98
U.S. Patent Trademark Office
    (USPTO), 101
University of Miami, 230
University of North Carolina,
    230
Urban-Think Tank, 186
USA Today, 31

video clips, 27–28
    in storytelling, 136
visual learning, vs. auditory,
    193
visuals, 220–221
    vs. art, 202, 205
    for big data, 33–34
    creators of, 227–228
    for data, 29–30, 33–34
    design guidelines, 205–208
    as distraction, 199
    learning to create, 230–231
    limitations, 207–208
    for presentations, 209–218
    quality of, 205
vocabulary
    acronyms, 80, 114–115
    big words, 111–112
    jargon, 80, 102
Vogel, Kathleen, 68–69
voice
    active vs. passive, 106
    see also human voice
volcanoes, 182

Walden (Thoreau), 88
Washington Post, 158, 225–227
weather, simulation, 34

web page
information on, vs. book, 37
links, 110
Westen, Drew, *The Political Brain*, 163
white papers, 154
White Space Is Not Your Enemy (Golombisky and Hagen), 231
Wikipedia, 81, 173
winnowing process, 94–95
wireless industry, competition, 162
Woodrow Wilson International Center for Scholars, 45, 133
World Intellectual Property Organization (WIPO), 145–147

writers
guidelines for working with, 84–85
locating, 85
writing, 7
first-person language, 121, 124
formality in, 153–154
formality of third person, 124
mechanized, 151
readability of, 103
writing skills, 83–84

Yergin, Daniel, *The Commanding Heights: The Battle for the World Economy*, 134
YouTube, 28, 136

Zimbalist, Michael, 198
zooms, 220

About the Author

Author, speaker, and consultant Frank J. Pietrucha understands the importance of communicating the complicated. He's helped clients explain their hard-to-grasp ideas, turning concepts that baffle into comprehensible ideas bosses, regulators, and investors embrace. He works with engineers, scientists, economists, lawyers and other smart people helping them mold their ideas into something non-specialists can comprehend. He's been "translating" on behalf of the technology elite for more than 20 years.

Pietrucha realized his talent for making complex topics easier to understand when organizing industry conferences on telecommunications, cyber security, mining, and financial services in the United States, Chile, and Brazil. At A.T. Kearney, a leading management consulting firm, and at The Launch Company, a public relations agency for high-tech start-ups, he honed his skills in de-geeking specialized topics. He started his own company, Definitive Communications, in 2001, working with clients such as George Washington University's Creative and Innovative Economy Center, the International Intellectual Property Institute, The Hartford, and NASA's Ames Research Center.

Realizing the significance of a changing communication landscape, he coined the term supercommunicator to describe a new breed of forward-thinking professional who can apply classic content-development skills to a mindset befitting the quickly evolving millennium. He continues to help clients explain their complicated concepts as a consultant and writer but is now more actively engaged in sharing his supercommunicator philosophy as a keynote speaker and workshop leader with people wishing to improve their communication skills.

Pietrucha earned a Bachelor of Arts degree from Cornell University. Additionally, he has completed course work at Universidad Iberoamericano in Mexico, University of Bath in England, and the School of Visual Arts. He resides on Capitol Hill in Washington, D.C.

BESTSELLERS FROM AMACOM

Lead with a Story: A Guide to Crafting Business Narratives That Captivate, Convince, and Inspire
ISBN: 9780814420300 (print) ISBN: 9780814420317 (ebook)

Forget facts, figures, and PowerPoint slides—well-crafted stories deliver business concepts simply and powerfully. The reason for this is simple: Stories have the ability to engage an audience the way logic and bullet points alone never could. Whether you are trying to communicate a vision, sell an idea, or inspire commitment, storytelling is a powerful business tool that can mean the difference between mediocre results and phenomenal success.

Just Listen: Discover the Secret to Getting Through to Absolutely Anyone
ISBN: 9780814414033 (print) ISBN: 9780814414040 (ebook)

Barricades between people become barriers to success, progress, and happiness, so getting through is not just a fine art, but a crucial skill. *Just Listen* gives you the techniques and confidence to approach the unreachable people in your life—and turn frustrating situations into productive outcomes and rewarding relationships.

Leading at The Edge: Leadership Lessons from the Extraordinary Saga of Shackleton's Antarctic Expedition, **Second Edition**
ISBN: 9780814431948 (print-paperback) ISBN: 9780814431610 (ebook)

In December of 1914, the British Imperial Trans-Antarctic Expedition, led by Sir Ernest Shackleton, sailed from the island of South Georgia in the Southern Ocean. Its goal: the first overland crossing of Antarctica. Soon trapped in a prison of solid pack ice, the crew became engaged in a legendary fight against brutal cold, impenetrable ice, dwindling food, and complete isolation. Despite these seemingly insurmountable obstacles, the team remained cohesive, congenial, and mercifully alive—a fact that speaks not just to luck but to an unparalleled feat of leadership.

Into the Storm: Lessons in Teamwork from the Treacherous Sydney to Hobart Ocean Race
ISBN: 9780814431986 (print) ISBN: 9780814431603 (ebook)

The iconic Sydney to Hobart Race, a 723-mile deepwater challenge—often called the "Everest" of offshore ocean racing—is considered one of the toughest in the world. Unpredictable weather and seas make each race demanding, but in 1998, an unexpected "weather bomb" hit the fleet, creating 80-foot waves and 100-mile-per-hour winds. Many bigger, better-equipped boats tried to maneuver around the storm, but the crew of the *AFR Midnight Rambler* chose to head directly into its path. After battling mountainous waves and hurricane-force winds in the Bass Strait, the tiny 35-foot boat arrived safely in Hobart, 3 days and 16 hours later—winning the coveted Tattersall's Cup. What were the factors underlying this incredible achievement? *Into the Storm* recounts the story of the Ramblers' stunning victory, and the teamwork that made it possible—revealing powerful lessons for success in today's demanding business environment.